The Strategic Role of Ukraine

T0334481

The Strategic Role of Ukraine

Diplomatic Addresses and Lectures
(1994–1997)

Yuri Shcherbak

Distributed by Harvard University Press
for the
Ukrainian Research Institute, Harvard University

Publication of this book has been made possible by the generous support of Daria Dudra, benefactor of Ukrainian studies at Harvard University.

ISBN 0-916458-85-7
This book has been printed on acid-free paper.

cover inset: Ambassador Yuri Shcherbak and President Bill Clinton, during Ambassador Shcherbak's presentation of his credentials in the White House, November 21, 1994.

Printed in Canada

The Ukrainian Research Institute was established in 1973 as an integral part of Harvard University. It supports research associates and visiting scholars who are engaged in projects concerned with all aspects of Ukrainian studies. The Institute also works in close cooperation with the Committee on Ukrainian Studies, which supervises and coordinates the teaching of Ukrainian history, language, and literature at Harvard University.

The Institute has established the series Harvard Papers in Ukrainian Studies as a medium for occasional papers, reports, reprints, long articles, and recent dissertations.

To my wife, Maria

Ambassador Yuri Shcherbak and President of Ukraine Leonid Kuchma, during
President Kuchma's visit to Washington, DC, February, 1996.

left to right: Maria Shcherbak, President of the United States Bill Clinton,
Hillary Rodham Clinton, and Ambassador Yuri Shcherbak, during
a diplomatic reception at the White House, January 1996.

Contents

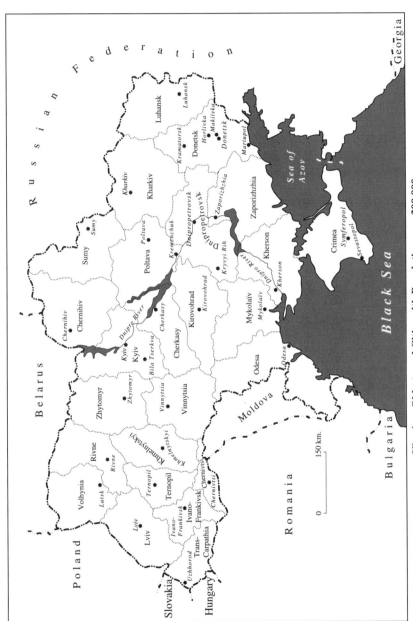

Ukraine: Oblasts and Cities with Population over 200,000

Preface

The basis of this book is a series of official addresses that I delivered between 1994 and 1997 while fulfilling my responsibilities as Extraordinary and Plenipotentiary Ambassador of Ukraine to the United States. Historically speaking, this is a quite short period. However, it has been extremely important for Ukraine precisely in terms of the historic activities that have occurred, both in international and domestic politics.

Leonid Kuchma became the president of Ukraine as the result of free and democratic elections in 1994. He announced a program of radical political and economic reforms and laid out a pragmatic, balanced course of international relations for the young Ukrainian government. This course has been aimed at the integration of Ukraine into Euro-Atlantic structures. Soon after the election, in November 1994, President Kuchma designated me to my current position. I presented my credentials to President Bill Clinton on the eve of the state visit of President Kuchma to the United States, which instituted a new level of friendship and cooperation between our two nations.

As the ambassador to the United States, I have had the occasion to take part in a series of important meetings, conferences, and symposia at which I have been able to present the official position of Ukraine. I also have been able to travel around this beautiful and grand country—from San Francisco to Boston, Salt Lake City to Cape Canaveral, from Houston to Detroit. Everywhere that I have gone, I have appeared before businessmen and students, scholars and journalists, and members of the Ukrainian-American community. I have attempted to discuss Ukraine as thoroughly and objectively as possible. I have presented to my audiences both Ukraine's achievements and its difficulties, and have laid out the foreign and domestic policy of my government.

Of course, the texts in this volume carry with them a trace of a biography that is unusual for a career diplomat. In them are elements of my experiences—as a medical doctor and epidemiologist, as a writer, as a member of the former Soviet Parliament (Supreme Soviet), as the minister of environment in the first government of independent Ukraine. And although the texts might at first glance appear to the reader to be a bit dry and guarded—as diplomatic texts tend to be—one must remember that they are in fact representative of the directives of the president of Ukraine and tightly controlled by instructions from the Ministry of Foreign Affairs. This does not constitute an arena in which the writer's imagination can be let loose or where the Green MP can supercede the bounds of the official foreign policy of Ukraine. Nevertheless, behind these "dry" texts are to be found the passions, struggle, and difficult work—day in and day out—of those to whom has fallen the great good fortune to create the history of a newly reborn Ukraine.

Seven years ago in Moscow (at that time I was a member of the USSR Supreme Soviet), my friend Alexey Yablokov, also an MP and famous ecologist, asked me, "Yuri, would you like to meet an American senator who will probably in the future become the president of the United States?" "Yes, sure," I answered. We met two Americans: a tall and very good-looking senator who took interest in ecological issues, and his beefy and curly-haired assistant. For more than two hours Alexey and I talked with our American guests about the catastrophic ecological situation in many areas of the Soviet Union. I told them what the situation was in Ukraine, especially after the Chornobyl disaster. The Americans listened very carefully. I said that the Soviet Union was facing dissolution and Ukraine, in my conviction, would soon become an independent state. This last statement was met by our guests with some mistrust.

Those American guests today are U.S. Vice-President Al Gore and his Assistant for National Security Issues Leon Fuerth. Every time I meet the Vice-President now, he recalls my forecast about Ukrainian independence.

America has been gracious to me. I have had the opportunity to meet with such luminaries of the highest echelons of politics here as President Clinton and former President George Bush; Secretaries of State Warren Christopher and Madeleine Albright; Secretaries of Defense William Perry and William Cohen; National Security Advisors Anthony Lake and Sandy Berger; Senators Bob Dole, Trent Lott, Jesse Helms, Mitch McConnell, William Roth, Jr., and Arlen Spector; Representatives Newt Gingrich, Porter Goss, John Fox, Sander Levin, Christopher Smith, David Bonior, and others. I take pride in the friendly relations that we have with such outstanding statesmen of the United States as First Deputy Secretary of State Strobe Talbott, who has played such a critical role in the formulation of the strategic policy of the Clinton Administration toward Ukraine. I also would like to express my appreciation for my colleagues at the Ukrainian Desk of the State Department, with whom I have been fortunate to work during these years: Ambassadors James Collins (now nominated to be U.S. ambassador to Russia), William Miller (my good partner, who served as U.S. ambassador to Ukraine), and Daniel Speckhard (now U.S. ambassador to Belarus); Jack Segal, Jon Purnell, Bruce Connuck, Nicholas Granias, and others. Close ties were also forged with the directors of the National Security Council: Steven Pifer (recently appointed U.S. ambassador to Ukraine), Coit Blacker, William Courtney, and Carlos Pascual, with whom I have had quite amicable relations. Thanks to their friendly attitude and deep understanding of the problems that Ukraine faces, we have been able to experience significant progress in the relationships between our two countries.

I also have been most fortunate in the friendship of one of Ukraine's greatest supporters, the world-renowned political thinker Zbigniew Brzezinski. Other experts in the field that I have had the pleasure of working with have included Sherman Garnett, Dimitri Simes, Paul Goble, Paula Dobriansky, Adrian Karatnycky, and John Mroz, among others. Of course, this book is not a narrative about these scholars, diplomats, and politicians, just as it does not attempt to describe America at the end of the 1990s. I do hope, however, that sometime in the future I will be able to address my thoughts along these lines in a more detailed—and less official—book. One of the chapters of this book will most certainly be dedicated to the Ukrainian-American community, its leading role in the attainment of independence in Ukraine, and its support for the young Ukrainian government. I have met many Ukrainian-Americans during my stay here and many have become friends—these wise and generous people—to whom I am boundlessly appreciative for their support of my work and that of the Embassy of Ukraine in the United States.

Every time I go to the State Department for talks or negotiations and go up to the seventh floor—to that triumphal interior, stylized in the manner of the late eighteenth and nineteenth centuries—to where the offices of the secretary and deputy secretary of state are, I walk down long corridors framed by the portraits of all of the former secretaries of state. I always try not to miss the portrait of Robert Lansing. I stand there, even if only for a moment, before this member of the Wilson Administration, who played no small role in the history of Ukraine. His role was not in the least positive. As strange as it might seem now, Lansing was resolutely set against the principle of national self-determination that was expounded by President Woodrow Wilson among his famous "Fourteen Points," which played a decisive role in the Paris Peace Conference in 1919 and 1920. As the Ukrainian historian Matvii Stakhiv has recently confirmed, "Lansing often concealed from Wilson intelligence reports that were favorable toward Ukraine and presented to Wilson only those that were unfavorable." Lansing, being an ardent Russophile, came out decisively in favor of the inviolability of the Russian Empire. Thus, at a session of foreign ministers at the Paris Conference on May 9, 1919, Lansing opposed even the *de facto* recognition of the Estonian government.[1] On behalf of the United States, he announced, "The

---

[1] Matvii Stakhiv, *Ukraïna v dobi Dyrektoriï UNR,* vol. 6, pp. 55–56 (notes 12, 19) and vol. 4, pp. 133–37 (esp. notes 215–17, 219) (Scranton, Pennsylvania, 1962–1966).

recognition of *de facto* governments on the territories which have belonged to Russia, would be to some measure a partition of Russia, and the United States has carefully avoided this, with the exception of Poland and Finland."[2] Who knows how world events might have evolved if the United States and other Allied governments had recognized the Ukrainian National Republic in 1918–19 and had given it support in the struggle against Russian Bolshevik aggression?

But history does not know the word "if." Gazing at the drawn visage of Lansing, with its grey moustache—this typical American statesman of the beginning of the twentieth century—I think to myself, "My God, how times have changed!" I think about the Joint Statement of the Ukraine-United States Binational Commission, which was signed on the May 16, 1997 by President Kuchma and Vice-President Gore. In it are the following words:

> The Sides underscored the importance of deepening cooperation to ensure the security interests of Ukraine and the United States, and to promote the integration of Ukraine as a central European state into European and Euro-Atlantic institutions. They affirmed that Ukraine should play a key role in ensuring peace and stability in Central and Eastern Europe and the continent as a whole.

On this optimistic note I would like to conclude and pass onto the reader these texts. There are two themes that run throughout them: first, the geostrategic, international role of Ukraine and the question of strengthening relations in the strategic partnership of Ukraine and the United States; and, second, a dynamic evaluation of the changes that are taking place in Ukraine in various spheres of life. My hope is that these pieces will enlighten and challenge the reader about the contemporary, complicated situation of a newly independent Ukraine.

Yuri Shcherbak
October 1997

---

[2]   Robert Lansing, *The Peace Negotiations. A Personal Narrative* (Boston, 1921).

Acknowledgments

In 1995 Professor George G. Grabowicz, then director of the Ukrainian Research Institute at Harvard University, asked me to deliver the Maria and Vasyl Petryshyn Memorial Lecture on the topic of "Ukraine's Foreign Policy and U.S.-Ukrainian Relations." I agreed to this, noting that it was a great honor for me to deliver a lecture at that world-renowned university. I also learned that the memorial lecture envisioned the publication of the text. However, at that time my responsibilities did not afford me the opportunity of working over the text for publication and I put the project onto a very back burner. I am deeply indebted to Professor Roman Szporluk, current director of the Institute, who in the spring of 1997 renewed the invitation for publishing the text and also expressed his desire not to limit the publication to the Petryshyn Memorial Lecture, but also to broaden and enrich it with the publication of other materials of mine.

Given my already over-subscribed schedule as ambassador, it would have been extremely difficult for me to finish this book, if not for the generous and thoughtful help of Robert De Lossa, director of publications for the Ukrainian Research Institute, whom I warmly thank. I also wish to thank all those in the Ukrainian Research Institute and the Embassy of Ukraine to the United States, who have helped make this book a reality.

Abbreviations

AGARD	Advisory Group for Aerospace Research and Development [NATO]
BSEC	Black Sea Economic Commonwealth
CEE	Central and Eastern European (Region)
CFE	Conventional (Armed) Forces in Europe (Treaty)
Cheka	Extraordinary Commission (for the Struggle against Counter-revolution and Sabotage) [early Soviet secret police; *Rus.* Chrezvychainaia komissiia]
CIS	Commonwealth of Independent States
CNAD	Conference of National Armaments Directors [NATO program]
CNFA	Citizens Network for Foreign Affairs [U.S.]
EFF	Extended Fund Facility [IMF loan type]
EU	European Union
GRU	(Soviet) Main Intelligence Directorate [*Rus.* Glavnoe razvedyvatel'noe upravlenie]
GSP	Generalized System of Preference
IMF	International Monetary Fund
KGB	Committee for State Security [Soviet secret intelligence agency; *Rus.* Komitet gosudarstvennoi bezopasnosti]
NACC	North Atlantic Cooperation Council
NATO	North Atlantic Treaty Organization
NIS	Newly Independent States
NKVD	People's Commissariat for Internal Affairs [a precursor of the KGB; *Rus.* Narodnyi komissariat vnutrennikh del]
NPT	(Nuclear) Non-Proliferation Treaty
OPIC	Overseas Private Investment Corporation [Independent U.S. federal agency]
OSCE	Organization for Security and Cooperation in Europe
PABSEC	Parliamentary Assembly of the Black Sea Economic Commonwealth
PfP	Partnership for Peace [NATO program]
START	Strategic Arms Reduction Treaty
STF	Strategic Transformation Facility [IMF loan type]
UADC	Ukrainian Agricultural Development Company
USAID	United States Agency for International Development
USIA	United States Information Agency
WB	World Bank
WEU	West European Union

The Strategic Role of Ukraine

The Strategic Importance of Ukraine

The proclamation of an independent Ukrainian state on the ruins of the Soviet Empire has changed the geopolitical reality of Europe and has drawn the close attention of political leaders, military specialists, political scientists, and all those engaged in strategic analysis and planning. Interest in Ukraine on the world stage is seen as early as the beginning of this century, especially in connection with the First World War. Max Weber, looking at the period of 1915 to 1919, ranked Ukraine among such "colonies" as Poland, Lithuania, Finland, India, Ireland, Malta, Egypt, Persia, and others, and was one of the champions of an independent Ukrainian state.[1] Between 1915 and 1918, Friedrich Naumann, a prominent German politician, advocated the concept of "Middle Europe" (Ger. *Mitteleuropa*), which implied a commonwealth or union of Central European States with an independent Ukraine as its member.[2] In Britain, the unique work carried out by the English researcher Lancelot Lawton and presented in February 1939 on the eve of the Second World War, reflects a profound understanding of Ukraine's role in the geopolitical stability of Europe. He stated:

> On the solution of the Ukrainian problem will depend the fate of Europe. Ukraine is from three to four times larger than and contains a population equal to that of Great Britain....Should such an attempt [as the independence of Ukraine] succeed, a nation would appear in Eastern Europe second only in size and population to Russia. So great an event would most likely be accompanied by, or cause remarkable changes elsewhere. It would influence, if not determine, the fate of Bolshevism and the Soviet Union.[3]

At the outset of Ukrainian independence in 1991 and 1992, its great strategic importance was underscored in this country by such prominent politicians and thinkers as Zbigniew Brzezinski, Henry Kissinger, and Strobe Talbott. Dr. Brzezinski's almost mathematically precise formula has become especially well known: "It cannot be stressed strongly enough that without Ukraine Russia ceases to be an empire, but with Ukraine suborned and then subordinated, Russia automatically becomes an empire."[4] Michael Mandelbaum shares this opinion:

> So long as it [Ukraine] remains independent, it is a buffer between Russia and the rest of Europe. More important, an independent Ukraine is the best guarantee that Russia will remain a peaceful nation-state. Conflict between the two would have adverse repercussions to the West. And if Moscow absorbed Ukraine or attempted to do so, Russia would again become a multinational empire, harboring a large, resentful subject nation with poor prospects for construction of a stable democratic system.[5]

In 1995, Strobe Talbott, now deputy secretary of state, stated that:

> ...the fate of Ukraine is key to stability in Central Europe—that if Ukraine could develop as an independent, sovereign nation, secure in its current borders, with normal, peaceful relations with its neighbors, then the entire region would have a better chance for peace and prosperity.[6]

Finally, on March 7, 1997, while greeting Ukrainian Foreign Minister Hennadiy Udovenko during his visit to Washington, Secretary of State Madeleine Albright noted that:

> Today, the United States and Ukraine are building a shared vision: a Europe at peace, fully integrated, and fully free. An independent, prosperous, and democratic Ukraine is a critical part of that vision. A democratic Ukraine will be an example to its neighbors and a leader throughout the region. A prosperous Ukraine will be a major world market and a strong contributor to the global economy. A peaceful Ukraine will be a vigorous partner in European and international affairs. The United States is committed to working with Ukraine to help achieve these goals in the months and years ahead.[7]

Statements about the "strategic," "key" role of Ukraine today, now that we move into our seventh year of independence, are incorporated in a number of NATO, OSCE, EU and other organizations' documents and have in actuality become a political maxim in a broad variety of forums. It is important to outline the features which in the past determined Ukraine's strategic role and continue to determine it today. Among the major factors which determine the geostrategic role of any country are the following:

1. Its geographic location, including the countries that surround it, its sea access, and land routes.

2. The size of the country and its natural relief.

3. Its population—including size, demographic characteristics, and ethnic composition, as well as its level of education and professional training.

4. Its natural resources—the availability of fossil fuels, water, arable land.

5. Its scientific, technological, industrial, military, and agricultural potential.

6. The availability of international trade routes crossing the country.

This list might be reinforced by a number of other important characteristics, including the present political and social system, quantitative and qualitative parameters of the armed forces, and the presence of weapons of mass destruction, to name a few. However, these six points provide a fairly universal standard for assessing the geostrategic importance of a country.

The criteria of the strategic importance for any country have always changed along with the history of mankind. While seven hundred years ago one of the major factors that incited the Mongol Tatar hordes to invade Kyivan Rus' was its affluent grazing lands (which might be compared to the quest for modern oil fields), for Hitler the main objectives were Donetsk coal, Ukrainian metal and grain, and the possibility of providing recreation centers for German troops in Crimea. It is quite possible that in the future, vital interests *vis–à-vis* Ukraine may be represented by as yet unknown mineral resources (new types of fuel and energy) or unique information technologies and other unforeseeable elements of future civilization.

The strategic importance of a country is also marked by the stability (or lack thereof) of its government and political-economic system. As John Jaworsky has remarked:

> Western commentaries frequently refer to a number of actual or potential threats to Ukraine's stability. These include continuing economic decline, which led to growing social distress and great dissatisfaction among the population; an increase in ethnic tensions and their potential transformation into communal conflict; centrifugal trends, sometimes linked to ethnic grievances, resulting in

autonomist or separatist movements; weak and distressed political institutions and widespread political apathy, which could leave the country open to the rise of authoritarian rulers or outside interference in its internal affairs; and a growth in tensions between Ukraine and Russia.[8]

Or as Heorhii Pocheptsov has put it, "The possibility of internal instability, for instance, from a deep economic crisis on top of an energy crisis is especially dangerous to Ukraine right now."[9]

Among the other measures of stability that can impact the strategic role of any country or society are non-material, but nonetheless important, spiritual and psychological indicators like the degree of national consciousness or the self-awareness and consolidation of the nation, factors which are difficult to quantify. Take Poland, for example: having ceased to exist as a state and having been three times partitioned by Russia, Prussia, and Austria-Hungary (1772, 1793, 1795)—and then further partitioned between Nazi Germany and the Soviet Union (1939–1941)—it still was able to re-establish a national state in 1918 and 1944, to a great extent because of the high degree of national-religious unity of Polish society.

On the basis of the above considerations, I would like, then, to review the basic strategic importance of Ukraine in 1997.

The Physical Geography of Ukraine

The first major consideration is the geographic location and the size of the country. Ukraine covers an area of 233,000 square miles. By comparison, France and Spain, respectively, occupy 212,900 and 195,900 square miles. The longest east-west distance in the country is 845 miles and the longest north-south distance is 555 miles (see map, p. viii). In the north Ukraine borders on Belarus; in the east and north-east on Russia; in the west it borders on Poland and Slovakia; and in the south-west it borders Hungary, Romania, and Moldova. The Ukrainian frontier is 4,040 miles long, with 650 miles of this being shoreline in the south (the Black Sea and the Sea of Azov).[10]

It is readily apparent from Ukraine's location that over the centuries it has been caught between the Russian Empire, the Polish-Lithuanian Commonwealth, Austria-Hungary, and the Ottoman Empire. Significant portions of contemporary Ukraine's territory have been included in these empires, and this has, to a large extent, determined the political history of the country. Historians have calculated that over the past millennium or so Ukraine has been the object of more than two hundred invasions, wars of aggression, or devastating occupations.

The country's wide expanses, natural riches, and the variety of its flora and fauna—all have been favorable conditions for the development of agriculture. At the same time, the moderate climate and large number of rivers and watersheds has made Ukraine one of the most strategically important and *attractive* regions in Central and Eastern Europe. This has been the case since the region's early history, but has been especially dramatic in the twentieth century. It is a little-known fact that Ukraine was one of the main, although carefully hidden, goals of the warring sides in World War I. In the first instance, it was precisely in western Ukraine that the most bloody battles of the eastern front were fought. This destroyed the local economy. Moreover, 3.5 million Ukrainians fought in the Russian Imperial Army, while 250,000 Ukrainians fought in the Austro-Hungarian Army, the majority of which perished.[11] Besides considerations of territory and manpower, Ukraine further occupied a special place in the plans of Austria-Hungary, Germany, and Russia. For instance, on November 20, 1914, the Austrian government sent a note to its allies, in which it declared, "the goal of Austrian politics in the war will be to wrest the Ukrainian people from Moscow and to establish an independent Ukraine. This will not only weaken Russia once and for all, but will also weaken its influence on the Black Sea basin."[12] Another example: At the beginning of the war, the German Chancellor Theobald von Bethmann-Holweg sent a memorandum to the German ambassador in Vienna in which he noted German desires to incite an uprising in Ukraine and to create a buffer zone consisting of Ukraine, the Congress Kingdom (Poland), the Baltic states, and the countries of the Caucasus.[13] Finally, on October 25, 1917, during a meeting between German Chancellor Georg Michaelis and General Berthenverfer, head of the political directorate of the German Army, it was determined that the army had to support German industrial interests in Ukraine. Again, the German politicians affirmed that the separation of Ukraine from Russia would weaken Russia in every way, would deny it access to the Balkans and Black Sea, and would facilitate a land route for Germany across the Balkans to the Near East.[14]

On the Russian side, one of its goals was to incorporate "Russian

Galicia" into the Empire, in order to annihilate the Ukrainian national movement that was located there. The Russian governor of Galicia, Count Georgii Bobrinsky, declared that, "Eastern Galicia and the Lemko territories have long been an integral part of Russia...I will introduce there the Russian language, law, and custom."[15]

Ukraine became one of the epicenters of the struggle between two cruel, totalitarian regimes during the Second World War. At the outbreak of the war, Germany was dependent on imports for fifty percent of its iron, obtaining it from Sweden, France, and Belgium. It also lacked sufficient supplies of non-ferrous metals, fuel, and foodstuffs.[16] Hitler believed that first and foremost these economic deficiencies must be overcome by occupying Ukraine, with the riches of the Donbas, and the Northern Caucasus. In this way he would secure plentiful grain supplies, coal, and oil. In a letter to Mussolini dated June 21, 1941 (that is, on the eve of his attack against the USSR), Hitler wrote, "Above all else, I hope that as a result of our success we will be able to secure a general supply base in Ukraine for a prolonged period. Ukraine will become for us a supplier of those resources that we will need in the future."[17]

In his memoirs, Marshal Georgii Zhukov wrote, "Stalin was convinced that in a war with the Soviet Union Hitler's forces would first try to take control of Ukraine with the Donbas in order to deprive our country of its most important economic regions and to seize Ukrainian grain, Donetsk coal, and then the oil of the Caucasus."[18]

The leadership of the Russian Empire and, in their turn, the leadership of the Soviet Union accorded Ukraine not only great economic significance, but also saw it as a great reservoir of human resources, on the one hand, and as a useful bridgehead for invading Europe. The popular writer Viktor Suvorov (whose real name is Volodymyr Bohdanovych Rezun; he is Ukrainian) has claimed in a carefully researched book that the Soviet Union actually prepared to make a preventative first strike against Germany in 1941. Suvorov—who at one time worked at the Soviet Main Intelligence Directory (GRU) at the General Headquarters of the Soviet Army—set forth a convincing set of figures and facts in order to show that Marshal Zhukov, the main proponent of the first strike policy, assigned a central role to the Lviv Strike Force of the Red Army. Armed forces, headquarters, communications lines, air fields, strategic reserves, and hospitals were all concentrated in this area. "The military understood the region from Lviv to Berlin to be one strategic corridor," writes Suvorov. "It would be impossible to repel a strike emanating from Lviv. Such a strike would not only put the Soviet forces into the industrial region of Silesia, but it would also cut Germany off from its oil reserves and its main allies…it would give the Soviets the opportunity to develop a march on Berlin or Dresden…It would cut off the German forces from their supply bases and from any industrial region." Zhukov also planned a strike into Romania. For this he proposed developing the Southern Front along the border with Romania.[19]

One can dispute Suvorov's theory about the planned strike through Ukraine against Germany, because in the end Germany struck first. However, the events of 1956 and 1968, with the invasions of Hungary and Czechoslovakia, respectively, prove the crucial role that the territory of Ukraine plays in the security of Europe. Suvorov shows that for the 1968 invasion two fronts were created—one called "Carpathian" and the other, "Central." Four armies were assigned to the Carpathian front. Two armies were sent through the narrow Soviet-Czechoslovak border (through Ukrainian territory; this border is now between Slovakia and Ukraine). Eleven divisions made up the two armies.[20]

Evaluating the possible military threats against Ukraine in the future, Professor Barry Posen of MIT underscores the fact that the geostrategic situation of Ukraine is vulnerable from the point of view of its long borders and its topographical relief. In his opinion, the Ukrainian landmass (the steppe and the large agricultural area) are especially useful for military action (and considers that the most serious threat to contemporary Ukraine can come from Russia). "This openness [of the territory]," he writes, "would provide excellent ground attack opportunities for a large, high technology airforce." The author, whose case is strengthened by the tragic events of World War II, underscores the fact that to the east of the Dnipro (Dnieper), there are, from a military standpoint, no substantial geographical barriers.[21]

Thus, while considering the entire complex of geographic and historical factors by which Ukraine occupies such an important place on the map of contemporary Europe, the concept of the unconditional maintenance of the territorial integrity of Ukraine becomes of utmost importance, as well as the inviolability of its borders, and the necessity of bilateral and reciprocal agreements to settle any territorial pretensions that one State might have against another.

Ukraine's Population and Ethnic Makeup

The population of Ukraine is 51.3 million people—46% male and 54% female—with 35.1 million living in urban areas and 16.2 million living in rural areas. The overall density for the entire country is 33 persons per square mile. The largest cities are Kyiv (population 2.6 million), Kharkiv (1.5 million), Dnipropetrovsk (1.1 million), Donetsk (1.1 million), Odesa (1.06 million), Zaporizhzhia (887.4 thousand), Lviv (805.9 thousand), Mykolaïv (519 thousand), and Luhansk (493.9 thousand).[22] Within Ukraine live some 128 nationalities and ethnic groups. The Ukrainian language is considered the mother tongue by 66.3% of the population, while 31.3% of the populace considers Russian its mother tongue.[23] The Ukrainian diaspora is between 10 and 13 million, with 7.7 million living in the countries of what was the USSR. In Russia alone, there are 4.3 million ethnic Ukrainians, the largest ethnic minority in the Russian Federation. In the United States there are approximately two million Ukrainian-Americans, while in Canada the number is put at about one million.[24]

During the twentieth century the population of Ukraine suffered tremendous demographic losses due to the two world wars, the civil war of 1917–1921, and the Stalinist repressions. During the period of the artificially induced famine of 1932–33, caused by the Bolsheviks, between seven and ten million people died. These were peaceful citizens, largely villagers.[25] In World War II, seven million Ukrainians served in the Red Army. Of these, 3.5 million perished.[26] Another 5.5 million Ukrainian non-combatants died during the war, so that Ukrainian losses during the war totaled nine million. The war lasted 1,220 days on Ukrainian territory. Seven hundred towns and 27,000 villages were destroyed. The Nazis forced 2.2 million Ukrainians into slave labor in Germany. They appropriated one-third of the entire GDP and took it out of the country by force.[27]

Normally, it would take 30 years to recover demographically from such losses. Unfortunately, beginning in the middle of the eighties, the demographic situation of Ukraine began once again to worsen. The total fertility rate fell to 1.7, while the infant mortality rate rose to 13.8 (by comparison, in the U.S. it is 9.1, in Japan—4.5, in Sweden—5.8).[28] Since 1991 there has been a net loss of population. Each year 170,000 to 300,000 more people die than are born.

Analysts also zealously note the regional variation of Ukraine, in which they divide the country into Crimea, with its primarily ethnic Russian population (67%); the western part of Ukraine, separate fragments of which in the past belonged to the Austro-Hungarian Empire, Poland, Romania, Czechoslovakia, or Hungary, and which are marked by a high level of national awareness and the adherence by a large portion of the population to the Greek-Catholic faith; and the south-east portion of the country, which is dominated by a Russophone Orthodox population. On the basis of this "regional differentiation," some have tried to utilize the theory of Samuel Huntington,[29] positing a "civilizational divide" that would appear to run down the middle of Ukraine, separating the eastern (Orthodox) part of the country from the western (Catholic) part. Ukraine is called a "multicivilizational" state with a large number of cultural and ethnic distinctions which lead to a lowered chance of the nation surviving as a whole, if the populace is able to exercise its rights in a democratic state.[30] In one particularly scandalous anonymous paper entitled "The CIS: The Beginning or End of History," a group of Russian analysts posited the unequivocal danger of Ukraine being divided by analogy with the period in the 17th century when it was divided between Poland and Russia (according to the Treaty of Andrusovo of 1667). In this and other position papers like it, aggressive voices have presented the split-up of Ukraine along the Dnipro River as almost a *fait accompli*.[31]

Yuri Lypa (1900–1944), an outstanding Ukrainian poet, historian, geopolitician, and soldier-physician in the Ukrainian Insurgent Army (UPA)—who was shot by Soviet counterintelligence units—considered the rending of Ukraine east from west to be the "most harmful doctrine for Ukraine...We can apply the 'East-West' doctrine to Ukrainian religious life—and we will have a religious war as a result," he said. "If we apply 'East-West' to politics, then we have a propitious field on which the agents of other powers will act against us."[32]

In a recent work by Tor Bukkvoll, which treats Ukraine in the context of European security, the author analyzes in detail the question of ethnic mobilization and separatism, paying special attention to the threat of separatism in Eastern and Southern Ukraine and Crimea. The author comes to the conclusion that, "the absence of ethnic mobilization among the Russians of Eastern and Southern Ukraine can be attributed only in part to the accomodating minority policy of the Ukrainian State and Moscow's policy of restraint."[33] Among other reasons for this absence of ethnic mobilization, the author mentions the fact that, "Russians in Ukraine are not seriously disadvantaged economically or politically" and also the fact that, "rational calculation of the anticipated costs and benefits of mobilizing for anti-independence [i.e., against Ukraine—Yu.S.]...leads many Russians of ESU [Eastern South Ukraine—Yu.S.] to the conclusion that the costs are too great. Fear of violent conflict, fueled in part by observation of separatists' experiences in other parts of the former Soviet Union and the risk of a return to old-style Communist politics, also figure in the calculations." With regard to the situation in Crimea, the author is more guarded in his prognosis: "Despite the successful suppression of Crimean separatism, Crimean ethnic passion is one of the most serious challenges to Ukrainian political stability."[34]

Precisely so. However, one most note that this analysis was made before the signing of the historic agreement between Ukraine and Russia and the final decision concerning the fate of Sevastopol as a Ukrainian city, in which, temporarily and on the basis of a treaty, the Russian Black Sea Fleet will be based. The future will show how strong and lasting this agreement will be.

Although the question of the possible ethnic or regional division of Ukraine is not directly a subject of the present work, I would note that this crudely mechanistic conception is deeply mistaken, because it does not take into account the great many political, economic, and social factors that have gone into state-building between 1991 and 1997 and which work toward the very real unification of the country. And there are many analysts, even in Russia, who, working on the basis of an objective analysis of contemporary Ukrainian reality, hold to this latter view and consider the chances of an east-west split in Ukraine unlikely.[35]

Natural Resources

Ukraine occupies only 0.45% of the Earth's dry land, but it boasts almost 5% of the world's mineral resources. There are extremely large deposits of hard coal, iron ore, manganese and titanium, and considerable deposits of mercury, chromite, aluminum, and nickel ores. Ukraine has potential reserves of oil and natural gas, which have come to the attention of foreign investors. Farming areas occupy 104 million acres, which include some of the finest black arable soils (*chornozem*) in the world.[36]

The Black Sea as a Factor

The Black Sea littoral is considered by a series of historians and political scientists to be one of the most important strategic factors in the overall security of Ukraine. This is due to the huge potential that exists for trade and economic ties with the countries of the Black Sea littoral as well as the Mediterannian and Near East. Mykhailo Drahomanov, the outstanding Ukrainian philosopher, publicist, and political advocate (1841–1895) wrote that, "Without the northern shores of the Black Sea it will be impossible for Ukraine to be a cultured country."[37] It is enough to look at a map of Ukraine to understand that the Crimean peninsula is critically important, since control of it means the effective defense of sea lanes in the region. In 1923, Stepan Rudnytskyi already wrote that, "The loss of Crimea [during the Civil War of 1917–1920—Yu. S.]... immediately condemned Ukrainian statehood to death. Without Crimea there is no independent Ukraine—its loss destroys Ukraine's main base and support, the Black Sea littoral."[38]

From earliest history, the area of the Black Sea littoral that falls within the territory of contemporary Ukraine has played an important strategic role in the structure of a broad international trade. The first Greek colonies appeared in this area 2,600 years ago, with settlements appearing in Olvia, Tiria (in the Dnister liman), Khersones (near modern Sevastopol), and Bosporus (near the Kerch peninsula). This area was occupied by Greece in order to secure grain for Athens. This reached its pinnacle out of Bosporus during the fourth century B.C. Experts estimate that the yearly export of grain from the Black Sea littoral was 16,700 tons. The littoral area also played an important part in the trade of slaves, cattle, fish, weapons, and handicrafts.

In the first century B.C. this area came under the Roman Empire, which exported material from it for the Roman Army. It is an interesting coincidence that in the very same place where we now have Sevastopol, two thousand years ago there was a Roman commander with a squadron and full garrison. In the fifth century A.D. this part of the Black Sea littoral came under the power of the Byzantine Empire, which accorded it great significance.[39] The Black Sea was not just a waterway for trade, but also proved to be a military route. Both the warriors of Kyivan Rus and the Zaporozhian Cossacks used it to attack Byzantium and Turkey.

Beginning in 1686, Muscovy attempted to conquer Crimea (the Crimean Khanate, which was an ally of Turkey), in order to have access to the Black Sea. The ultimate goal of the Russian Empire was to control the Bosporus and Dardanelles Straits in order to gain an outlet to the Mediterannean Sea. The path to Crimea lead through Ukraine, inflicting upon its inhabitants a long history of suffering. Ukrainian Cossacks also took part in the wars for Crimea at a level equal to the Russian forces. Russia occupied the Crimean peninsula in 1774 and in 1783 it annexed the Crimean Khanate to the Russian Empire.[40] The Crimean Khanate, which had been a strong and wealthy state during the 15th to 17th centuries and had played an important part in Ukrainian history, was destroyed. Of an original population of 4 million Tatars, after 130 years of agressive rule on the part of Russia only 150,000 remained in the Crimean highlands and mountains. Hundreds of thousands of Crimean Tatars were forced by the Russian authorities to emigrate to Turkey in order to salvage their faith, traditions, and culture.[41]

In 1944 Stalin decreed that the entire Crimean Tatar people had been involved in treason to the Fatherland and had crossed over *en masse* in support of the Nazi occupiers. For this he ordered the entire population of 238,000 souls to be deported to the Asiatic republics of the USSR. In the course of the six-month long deportation as many as 110,000 people died.[54]

After WWII, the Soviet Union, fighting for domination over the Black Sea and Mediterranean Sea basins turned the Black Sea Fleet, based not only in Sevastopol, but all along the Soviet Black Sea coast, into an operational and strategic force of 100,000 men with 700 warships and support vessels, some with tactical nuclear weapons. In case of WWIII, Soviet troops based in Ukraine and Moldova were to occupy the northern shore of the Bosporus, while troops stationed in Georgia and Armenia would take the southern shore. The Black Sea Fleet was seen as the main neutralizing force against the U.S. Sixth Fleet, based in the Mediterranean.[43]

The dissolution of the USSR and the declaration of independence on the part of Ukraine—of which Crimea and Sevastopol are integral parts—initiated a lengthy conflict between Russia and Ukraine concerning the division and basing of the Black Sea Fleet.[44] The current naval forces of Ukraine comprise 100 warships and support vessels, which are strengthened by cooperation with the countries in the Black Sea region and NATO. These forces take part in joint exercises along with ships from the U.S., Turkey, Italy, Greece, Romania, and other countries. In 1997 the joint exercises known as "Sea Breeze 1997" and the Ukrainian-British-Polish joint exercises known as "Cossack Steppe 1997" took place with the participation of airborne troops.

The change in the geostrategic situation in the region of the Black Sea has raised sharp concerns among Russian military officials and politicians, who denounce the activity of Turkey, the U.S., and other NATO countries in the region. According to Admiral Viktor Kravchenko, who commands the Russian Black Sea Fleet, "Russia cannot be weakened in this region." According to him, in the past two years NATO warships have spent 400 days in the region, collecting hydrotopographic and radio-location information.[45]

Outside of the military-strategic role that the Black Sea plays, the existence of the large Ukrainian port-cities of Odesa, Kherson, Mykolaïv, Kerch, Sevastopol, and Izmaïl now creates sizeable opportunities for the development of marine passenger and freight routes and increased international trade. Ukraine actively participates with the other Black Sea countries in the PABSEC (Parliamentary Assembly of the Black Sea Economic Commonwealth). Of strategic importance is the creation of a ferry line from Odesa to Poti in Georgia, which will become one of the links in the Trans-Caucasus Corridor for the transport of Caspian oil from Azerbaijan across the territory of Georgia to the port of Odesa. Odesa is currently constructing an oil terminal to receive large oil freighters. Significant opportunities have also been opened by Ukraine's participation in the building of the Ceyhan-Samsun oil pipeline in Turkey, from which oil will be transported by tanker to Odesa and from there to Poland through the Odesa-Brody pipeline.

Industrial-Scientific Potential

Ukraine is a developed industrial-agricultural country. In 1890 seventy percent of the Russian Empire's pit coal and fifty-one percent of its cast iron were extracted in Ukraine. At the beginning of the century, Ukraine had developed heavy industry, including coal mining technologies, metallurgy, sugar manufactures, agricultural machine-building, steamship manufacture, and marine ship building. The manufacture of cast iron and steel was concentrated in eighteen large metallurgical factory complexes, from which flowed nearly three million tons of metal in 1914. In some two hundred Ukrainian sugar plants production met nearly eighty percent of the total consumption of the Russian Empire.[46] Within the Soviet Union on the eve of its dissolution, Ukraine contributed seventeen percent of total industrial production, including forty percent of Soviet steel, thirty-four percent of its coal, and fifty-one percent of its cast iron.[47] At present, Ukraine produces one-tenth of the world's cast iron, one-eleventh of its steel, and one-twelfth of its pit coal. Heavy industry, especially ferrous metallurgy, coal, and machine-building, continue to be prominent in the national industrial complex. The military industrial complex also continues to occupy an important place in the national economy.

Attainments of the "Southern" (Ukr. *Pivdenny*) Machine-building Plant complex and the Southern Design Bureau are known far outside Ukraine. This facility is the largest rocket manufacturer in the world and during the Soviet period produced ICBMs, like the SS-24. Now, this facility is cooperating with the U.S., Russia, and Norway, within the parameters of the "Sea Launch" project, for the commercial launch of space satellites. Aircraft of Ukrainian manufacture are also well known. Models developed by the Antonov Aviation Research and Technology Complex, like the An-22 (Antei), An-32, An-124 (Ruslan), An-225 (Mriya), and An-70, are built in Kyiv and Kharkiv.

At present the National Academy of Sciences of Ukraine comprises 170 research centers, including five international venues with powerful research and production facilities. Sixty-one thousand people are employed by the Academy of Science, including over 46,000 researchers. The Academy includes 203 academicians and 280 corresponding members, including eighty-one foreign members from eighteen countries, including the U.S., France, Germany, the U.K., Italy, Russia, and Japan. The Academy ranks among the leading scientific venues of Europe. In a series of fields, like high-technology electrical welding, rocket building, cybernetics, mathematics, genetics, and materials science, Ukrainian scientists occupy world-class, leading positions.[48] The high level of education of the Ukrainian populace and the country's scientific development will facilitate Ukraine in the future as one of the leading sites in the world for technological advancement.

Agriculture

Ukraine has long been known as the breadbasket of Europe. Throughout its history, the "productivity factor" (the provision of foodstuffs grown on arable lands) has acted as an important stimulus for aggression from all directions. It is worthwhile noting that at the beginning of the twentieth century ninety percent of *all* Russian exports (which equals one hundred percent of all *grain* exports) came from Ukraine. At the time, Ukraine harvested forty-three percent of the world's barley, twenty percent of its wheat, ten percent of its corn.[49] Additional important crops included sugar beets and tobacco.

During the First World War and the Civil War, Ukrainian grain became a strategically important product for a series of governments and regimes. In 1918, the Austrian Eastern Army, consisting of four corps and two divisions, and the German Occupation Army, consisting of twenty divisions, were located on Ukrainian territory. These forces were tasked with the expropriation of agricultural products from Ukraine. There is a famous telegram from the Austrian government to its representative in Kyiv, Count Forgach (April 3, 1918), in which the government informed him that Austria faced imminent famine, unless 50,000 wagonloads of grain could be brought from Ukraine.[50]

The cruelest forms of expropriation were the requisitions of Ukrainian grain carried out by the Bolshevik "foodstuff detachments," sent on orders by Lenin. There is a well-known dispatch from Lenin dated January 15, 1918, in which he says, "For god's sake, apply the most energetic and revolutionary methods for extracting grain, grain, and more grain!!! Otherwise, Piter [i.e., St. Petersburg, then the capital of Soviet Russia—Yu.S.] will die. Arrange for special trains. Organize collection and accumulation in central points. Make sure the trains are accompanied. Keep me informed daily. For god's sake! Lenin."[51]

According to far-from-complete statistics, in 1918 eighty-six wagonloads of sugar were taken from the Poltava region to Russia, 1,090 wagonloads of grain from the Kherson region, and 1,700 wagonloads of grain from the Kharkiv region.[52] As a result of these requisitions and the general destruction of the Civil War, famine arose in 1921 and 1922. During this famine hundreds of thousands of people perished.

Full and all-encompassing control by the Soviet regime of Ukrainian agricultural production occurred as a result of a terrible campaign to collectivize private farms between 1927 and 1934. This was a true war between the Stalinist regime and the peasantry, which led to countless victims during the Stalinist Terror Famine.[53]

Today, agriculture in independent Ukraine is a constant factor in the stability of the government and is an important component in Ukraine's exports. Farming areas occupy 104 million acres of land (while Ukraine *in toto* has 148 million acres of dry land). Arable land stands at 82.2 million acres. Statistically, each family in the country has 11.1 acres of farmland. Upwards of four million people are employed in the agrarian sector. In 1994 crop yields were: 35.5 million tons of grain, 28.1 million tons of sugar beets, 1.7 million tons of oil-bearing plants, and 5.1 million tons of vegetables.[54]

Intersections

Ukraine lies at a crossroads, which for centuries has been an important strategic factor determining the significance of the land. During the period of Kyivan Rus' (9th–12th centuries) three main international routes passed through the area: 1) the north-south route known as "from the Varangians to the Greeks," i.e., from Scandinavia to Byzantium, going down the Dnipro to the Black Sea and on to Constantinople; 2) the Salt Route (from the south along the Dnipro to the west in Galicia); and 3) the Iron Route (going from the south along the Dnipro to the east to the Sea of Azov and on to the Caucasus).[55] Kyivan Rus' supplied fur, wax, honey, hides, weapons (swords and suits-of-mail), dyes, and slaves. From Byzantium, Rus' got gold, silver, fine cloth, wine, and oil. From the Arab East it imported fine dishes and vessels and dyes.[56]

Yuri Lypa, mentioned above, considered the fundamental axis of Ukraine to be north-south, not east-west. He saw this axis cutting through the central Dnipro basin, corresponding essentially to the ancient trade route known as the path "from the Varangians to the Greeks."[57] It is noteworthy that the idea of a Baltic-Black Sea alliance, that would include Ukraine, Poland, the Baltic countries, Romania, Moldova, Bulgaria, Georgia, Turkey, and others arose in the early 1990s and was announced as a political idea in 1994 in Kyiv at the Intersea Parties Conference.[58]

Throughout the ages Ukraine has been a favorable location for trade.

It suffices to look at the present map of Ukraine to understand the beneficial geographical position that it occupies, being a central nexus for the transport of people, products, and capital. At present, Ukraine has 14,200 miles of operational rail lines and 101,000 miles of roads. Ukraine is traversed by a number of international highways (for example, Ukraine-Poland-Hungary-Romania-Slovakia; Ukraine-Russia; Ukraine-Belarus-Baltic States).[59] Ukraine also has great potential as an international stopover for flights from Europe to Asia and from Northern Europe to the Near East.

This has been a far from complete listing of factors of the strategic importance of Ukraine, however, the political history of our people attests to the fact that Ukraine occupies a crucial place in the Central and East European region. It is not without reason that such a thought-provoking political scientist as Sherman Garnett wrote recently that:

> Ukraine is the keystone in the arch of the emerging security environment in Central and Eastern Europe. It is a state that is too large and too geographically central to this emerging security environment to be ignored. Key issues of Russia's own long-term evolution are bound up in its relations with Ukraine. Russia's definition of itself as a state and international actor is significantly shaped by its long-term ties with Ukraine. It is a matter of particular importance, whether a new era of normal state-to-state relations can replace a long and complicated history of Kyiv's subordination to Moscow. Whether Russian led integration on the territory of the former USSR will pose a serious, long-term military challenge to the West, depends in large part on the role that Ukraine plays or is compelled to play within the Commonwealth of Independent States.[60]

Reviewing these questions concerning the strategic importance of Ukraine, we have looked at the facts of the past, often turning to dramatic examples from the First and Second World Wars.

At the same time, casting a purely military eye on these matters—looking only down a barrel and through cross-hairs, as it were—is in my opinion an anachronism on the threshold of the twenty-first century. Lord Salisbury put it quite cleverly when he said, "I would not be too much impressed by what the soldiers tell you about the strategic importance of…places. If they were allowed full scope they would insist on the importance of garrisoning the moon in order to protect us from Mars."[61]

At the end of the twentieth century, when the threat of global nuclear war has diminished as a result of the fall of the Soviet Union and to a great measure because Ukraine decided to remove from its territory its nuclear weapons, new strategic challenges arise of a non-military character: the globalization of trade, the telecommunications revolution, and the development of new technologies, which are beginning to play an ever greater strategic role in those countries that are united by great trade and economic alliances, on the model of the EU, NAFTA, and others.

In order to preserve its sovereignty and to strengthen its strategic significance in Europe, Ukraine needs core modernization, the destruction of old Soviet stereotypes and habits, and the decisive activiation of the process of strengthening its integration into Euro-Atlantic structures. As has been noted recently in a book prepared by the National Institute of Strategic Studies (Kyiv), entitled *The National Security of Ukraine, 1994–1996,* the most serious threats to Ukraine are "internal ones, first and foremost in the economic sphere." The authors make the following observation:

> The main priority of the nation is the creation of a contemporary market economy, which is integrated into the international economic system. In the social sphere the national priority of equivalent significance is the formation of a middle class as the basis for a reformed society.[62]

The future of Ukraine depends on the resolution of these problems. History is not a scientific experiment, the results of which can be calculated and foreseen. The most rational and pragmatic minds stop before the unknown, which is called simply the Future. We do not know what will happen tomorrow or ten years from now. But we can see the tendencies that are developing, for we swim in a wide river called Time and we can guess where its currents will take us.

Notes to the Introduction

1. Vadym Levandovs'kyi, "Ukraine in Geopolitical Concepts of the First Third of the 20th Century," *Politychna dumka/Political Thought* 1994 (3): 62–63.

2. Ibid., pp. 60–61.

3. Lancelot Lawton, "Ukraine: Europe's Greatest Problem," *East Europe and Contemporary Russia* 3(1) Spring 1939: 3–4. [Reprinted November, 1950.]

4. Zbigniew Brzezinski, "The Premature Partnership," *Foreign Affairs* 72(2) March–April 1994: 80.

5. Michael Mandelbaum, "Preserving the New Peace. The Case Against NATO Expansion," *Foreign Affairs* 74(3) May–June 1995: 10–11.

6. Strobe Talbott, "US Interests and Russian Reform," State Department *Dispatch* 6(10) 1995.

7. Cited from "Building a Partnership with Ukraine." Address by Jack D. Segal, Director, Western Slavic Affairs, Department of State, March 21, 1997.

8. John Jaworsky, "Ukraine: Stability and Instability," *McNair Papers* 42 (August 1995): 2.

9. Heorhii Pocheptsov, *Natsional'naia bezopasnost' stran perekhodnogo perioda.* Kyiv: Ministerstvo Osvity Ukraïny, 1996, p. 26.

10. *This is Ukraine.* Kyiv: Computer Systems, 1995, p. 7.

11. Orest Subtelny [Subtel'nyi], *Ukraïna. Istoriia.* Kyiv: Lybid', 1992, p. 296.

12. Isydor Nahaievs'kyi, *Istoriia ukraïns'koï derzhavy dvadtsiatoho stolittia.* Kyiv: Ukraïns'kyi pys'mennyk, 1993, pp. 53–54.

13. M. Nesun, V. Repryntsev, Ie. Kamins'kyi, "Ukraïna u zarubizhnykh doktrynakh ta stratehiiakh XX stolittia," *Politychna dumka/Political Thought* 1995 (2–3) 6: 51.

14. Ibid.

15. Nahaievs'kyi, *Istoriia ukraïns'koï derzhavy*, p. 56.

16. P. A. Zhilin, *Kak fashistskaia Germaniia gotovila napadenie na Sovetskii Soiuz.* Moscow: Mysl', 1966, p. 92.

17. Ibid., p. 200.

18. G. A. Zhukov, *Vospominaniia i razmyshleniia.* Moscow: APN, 1970, p. 220.

19. Viktor Suvorov [Volodymyr Bohdanovych Rezun], *Den' "M".* Kyiv: Zoloti vorota, 1994, pp. 213–15.

20. Viktor Suvorov [Volodymyr Bohdanovych Rezun], *Osvoboditel' (Rasskazy osvoboditelia).* Cherkassy: RIA "Ird Ltd.," 1995, p. 208.

21. Barry Posen [B. Pozen], "Kontseptsiia oborony dlia Ukrainy," in *Ukraina: problemy bezopastnosti.* Moscow: Moscow Carnegie Center, 1996, pp. 88–89. [=*Nauchnye doklady,* vyp. 12.]

22. *This is Ukraine,* pp. 14, 30.

23. Orest Deichakiwsky, "National Minority in Ukraine," *Ukrainian Quarterly* 50(4) 1994: 371–89.

24. *Ukraïns'ka diaspora u sviti. Dovidnyk.* Kyiv: Znannia, 1993, p. 18.

25. Andrea Graziosi. *The Great Soviet Peasant War. Bolsheviks and Peasants, 1917–1933.* Cambridge, Mass.: Ukrainian Research Institute, 1996, p. 4.

26. *Povidomlennia Ukrinform* June 18, 1997.

27. *Povidomlennia Ukrinform* September 14, 1994.

28. Oleh Wolowyna. *Ukraine: A Country in Transition. Demographic Implications for Socio-Economic Development at the Oblast' Level.* Durham: Center for International Development Research Triangle Institutue, 1994.

29. Developed in Samuel Huntington, *The Clash of Civilizations and the Remaking of World Order.* New York : Simon & Schuster, 1996.

30. Sergei M. Samuilov, "O nekotorykh amerikanskikh stereotipakh v otnoshenii Ukrainy," *SSha-ÈPI* 1997 (3–4): 87; and, Vladimir A. Kolosov, "Perspektivy rossiisko-ukrainskikh otnoshenii," *Nezavisimaia gazeta* 13 February 1997.

31. "SNG: nachalo ili konets istorii," *Nezavisimaia gazeta* 26 March 1997. On the Treaty of Andrusovo, see Zbigniew Wójcik, *Traktat Andruszowski 1667 roku i jego geneza.* Warsaw: PIW, 1959.

32. Yuri Lypa. *Pryznachennia Ukraïny.* 2nd ed. New York: "Howerla," 1953, p. 285. [First edition = 1938.]

33. Tor Bukkvoll, "Ukraine and European Security." *Hatam House Papers.* London: Royal Institute of International Affairs, 1997, pp. 44–45.

34. Ibid.

35. A. Moshets, "Rossiisko-ukrainskie otnosheniia v period do 2000 goda," in *Rossiia i ee sosedi. Nauchnye doklady Moskovskogo tsentra Karnegi.* Moscow: Moscow Carnegie Center, 1995, p. 51.

36. *This is Ukraine,* p. 19.

37. Oleksandr Soltans'kyi. "Heopolitychni siuzhety v Ukraïns'kyi suspil'nii dumtsi (persha polovyna XX stolittia)." *Politychna dumka* 1996 (1): 86.

38. Ibid., p. 90.

39. I. I. Artemenko (ed.) et al. *Istoriia Ukraïns'koï RSR,* vol. 1, pt. 1, pp. 187–217. Kyiv: Naukova dumka, 1977.

40. Subtelny, *Ukraïna,* p. 161.

41. M. N. Hubohlo and S. M. Chervonnaia. *Krymskotatarskoe natsiolal'noe dvizhenie,* vol. 1, pp. 50, 70. Moscow: Russian Academy of Sciences, 1992. *See also,* Ozenbashly, "Rol' tsarskogo pravitel'stva v èmigratsii krymskix tatar." *Krym* 1926 (2): 143–46.

42. Hubohlo and Chervonnaia, *Krymskotatarskoe,* pp. 80–81.

43. "Sud'ba Chernomorskogo flota." *Nezavisimaia gazeta* 1996 (45) 8 August: Appendix. *See also,* T. Kasimova, "Kuda poplyvet Chernomorskii flot?" *Zerkalo* (Baku) 31 August 1996.

44. "Developments in Crimea." *Challenges for Ukraine and Implications for Regional Security. An Internal Conference.* Kyiv, 23–25 October 1994.

45. Interfaks communication, 22 January 1997.

46. S. M. Korolivskii, M. A. Rubach, and N. I. Suprunenko, *Pobeda sovetskoi vlasti na Ukraine.* Moscow: Nauka, 1967, pp. 13–15.

47. Subtelny, *Ukraïna.*

48. *This is Ukraine,* p. 219.

49. Subtelny, *Ukraïna.*

50. Isydor Nahaievs'kyi. *Istoriia ukraïns'koï derzhavy dvadtsiatoho stolittia.* Kyiv: Ukraïns'kyi pys'mennyk, 1993, pp. 122–23.

51. V. I. Lenin, *Polnoe sobranie sochinenii,* 5th ed., vol. 50, p. 30. Moscow: Gosudarstvennyi izdatel'stvo politicheskoi literatury, 1970.

52. Korolivskii et al., *Pobeda sovetskoi vlasti,* pp. 494–97.

53. Robert Conquest. *The Harvest of Sorrow. Soviet Collectivization and the Terror Famine.* New York: Oxford University Press, 1986. *See also,* Graziosi *The Great Soviet Peasant War.*

54. *This is Ukraine,* p. 247.

55. Ivan M. Hapusenko, *Borot'ba skhidnykh slov'ian za vykhid do Chornoho moria.* Kyiv: Naukova dumka, 1966, pp. 55–56.

56. Artemenko (ed.) et al., *Istoriia,* vol. 1, pt. 1, p. 291.

57. Lypa, *Pryznachennia Ukraïny,* pp. 286–87.

58. *Intersea Bulletin. Countries of the Baltic-Black Sea-Adriatic Region.* League of Parties, no. 1 (August 1994). Kyiv: Ukraïns'ka Respublikans'ka partiia, 1994.

59. For further details, see *This is Ukraine,* p. 249.

60. Sherman Garnett, *Keystone in the Arch. Ukraine in the Emerging Security Environment of Central and Eastern Europe.* Washington, DC: Carnegie Endowment for International Peace, 1997, p. 7.

61. *The Diplomat's Dictionary.* Comp. Charles W. Freeman, Jr. Washington, DC: NDU Press, 1994, p. 284.

62. *Natsional'na bezpeka Ukraïny, 1994–1996 rr.* Kyiv: Rada Natsional'noï Bezpeky i Oborony Ukraïny, 1997.

ONE

Ukraine's Foreign Policy and U.S.-Ukrainian Relations*

I remember very well the morning in March 1953 when I, then a first-year student at Kyiv Medical High School, was standing on Khre-shchatyk Street, the main street of the city of Kyiv. A crowd of many thousands of Kyivites filled the streets and squares around. People were gloomy, many were crying. Red banners with black mourning ribbons were carried.

It was the day that Stalin died, the dictator who had ruled the largest empire in the world stretching from Beijing to Warsaw, from Hanoi to Berlin. It was the time when the Korean War was escalating. The nuclear arms race had just been initiated. Millions of people in the USSR and so-called "people's democracy" countries were prisoners in concentration camps. The people were afraid of their future, scared of the possibility of the breakout of nuclear war. Ukraine still was a constituent part of the Soviet empire and everyone thinking of its independence could find himself in the Gulag.

And here today, at the end of the 20th century, I, as ambassador of independent Ukraine, have the honor to present to you my thoughts on the current problems of Ukraine's foreign policy and U.S.-Ukrainian relations. Speaking about Ukraine's foreign policy and U.S.-Ukrainian relations—thinking of the future—we should always remember about the past, about our history.

The two factors which to a large extent determine the destiny of peoples and states are geography and history. Ukraine has a unique and key location in Europe irrespective of its name— whether it is Kyivan Rus or the Ukrainian People's Republic, a province of the former Russian or Soviet Empires, or just "Ukraine," irrespective of forms of government or state structure. Over the centuries, Ukraine has often

---

* The Vasyl and Maria Petryshyn Memorial Lecture in Ukrainian Studies (Harvard University, April 21, 1995).

become the object of aggression and occupation from all directions—
from east and west, from north and south. In the thirteenth and four-
teenth centuries the disintegration of the mighty Kyivan Rus state was
accelerated by the Tatar-Mongol invasion. Hundreds of times the fiery
waves of war and occupation have coursed through the territory of
Ukraine.

In the 20th century, Europe has experienced three major historic
turning points: the fall of the Russian, Austro-Hungarian, German and
Turkish Empires as a result of the First World War; the dissolution of
the aggressive Nazi Germany bloc at the end of the Second World War
and the re-division of the post-war world in Yalta; the fall of the Soviet
empire as a result of its defeat in the "Cold War," the emergence of a
number of New Independent States and a dramatic change in the political image of the world.

All these events directly affected Ukraine's fate. During the First
World War, major battles on the eastern front took place on the territory of western Ukraine. The revolution of 1917–1918 proclaimed state
independence of Ukraine which was subsequently occupied by German,
Austrian, French, Polish, White Guard (Czarist Russian), and Communist forces and became the arena of brutal civil war for 5 years. The fight
ended with the victory of Bolsheviks and subsequent formation of the
Union of Soviet Socialist Republics, with Ukraine becoming a part of it.

During the second World War, Ukraine fell victim to German aggression and lost nine million of its citizens and half of its industrial potential. Unfortunately, during the Cold War Ukraine twice became the
bridgehead for Soviet aggression: against Hungary in 1956 and against
Czechoslovakia in 1968.

The dissolution of the Soviet Union and Ukraine's proclamation of
state independence on August 24, 1991 became one of the most important global historic events of the 20th century and radically changed the
map of Europe. From the first days of its independent existence, the new
Ukrainian state—proceeding from its own interests for guaranteeing its
national security, and consolidating its sovereignty, independence and
territorial integrity—began to pursue an active foreign policy. In this
regard, we had to find our geostrategic place in the world and in Europe,
to realistically define our possibilities and goals. We also had to adjust
the psychological stereotypes of old Soviet thinking. The old Communist elite and many so-called "ordinary people" had identified them-

selves within the framework of a huge superpower called the USSR, which stretched between Japan and Poland, between Finland and Afghanistan. The empire dissolved but such thinking still haunts us. This phenomenon reminds me, a medical doctor, of so-called "phantom pain"—imaginary pains that a person suffers in his legs although, both legs have been amputated long ago.

For many politicians and analysts in the world the breakup of the Soviet Empire and emergence of independent Ukraine came as a true shock. But those who know well the history of Ukraine and apply a systematic and objective approach to politics and economics understand that such dramatic events do not occur all of a sudden, they ripen step by step in the depths of the past.

Let me return to the past and review a very important event on Ukraine's road to its real statehood.

On August 22, 1945, almost to a day forty-six years before Ukraine's independence was proclaimed, the Presidium of the Supreme Soviet (Parliament) of Ukraine ratified the United Nations Charter signed in San Francisco by the Ukrainian delegation on July 27, 1945. Thus, the Ukrainian Soviet Socialist Republic became a founding member state of the United Nations. None of the participants of this memorable event— the Soviet leaders Stalin, Molotov, Khrushchev, Manuilsky, U.S. President Truman, British Prime Minister Churchill and other officials could have imagined what historic and global significance this event would acquire in the future.

In accordance with Stalin's strategy to glean as many international and political benefits as possible from the victory in the Second World War, on February 1, 1944 the Soviet Constitution was changed to include an amendment to Article 18A stating that every Soviet Republic "has the right to enter into direct relations with foreign states to conclude agreements and exchange diplomatic and consular representatives with them." Stalin, the cruel, self-confident and powerful dictator of the Soviet empire, of course was not aware that he was placing a timebomb underneath the infrastructure of the USSR, by establishing a possibility for the enslaved quasi-state Ukraine to become in the future a full-fledged member of the international community.

It is from 1945 that a new stage in Ukraine's international activities began, when it became one of the important players in the consciousness of the United Nations, though it continued to exist only as a semi-state within the framework of the Soviet Union. It is under these conditions of Ukraine's membership in the United Nations that its diplomatic service began to take shape, and missions were sent to New York, Geneva, Paris, Vienna. The Ministry of Foreign Affairs established in 1944 began to play a key role as an important factor of the future state independence of Ukraine. For comparison: if at the beginning Ukraine's Foreign Ministry employed only 60 diplomats and about 40 technical staff, today it accounts for 560 positions, including about 300 in diplomatic posts in Ukraine and abroad. Today Ukraine has 25 embassies and seven consulates general, and in all there are 55 foreign missions of Ukraine in 43 countries of the world. Our country has established diplomatic relations with 130 countries around the world. It has been recognized by over 150 countries.[1] Ukraine is now a member of about 40 interstate organizations, having doubled its participation in the last two years.

On July 2, 1993 the Supreme Rada (Parliament) of the new independent Ukraine adopted the "Guidelines of Ukraine's Foreign Policy." In it Ukraine articulates its potential to become an influential regional power, to play an important role in maintaining political and economic stability in Europe. The pursuit of peace and stability internationally, and of well-being domestically, are Ukraine's major goals.

Ukraine is pursuing an open foreign policy and is striving for cooperation with all interested parties while avoiding dependence on individual states or groups of states. The relations which Ukraine develops are based on the principles of mutual advantage and non-interference in domestic affairs. Ukraine is not an enemy of any state, it condemns war as a means of national policy and abides by the principle of the non-use of force. We have no territorial claims against our neighbors but will not accept any territorial claims against us.

In 1994 as a result of free democratic elections President Leonid Kuchma became the second president of Ukraine. The period of political romanticism and economic stagnation, self-isolation and absence of practically any reforms came to an end.

In his speech at the 49th UN General Assembly (1994) Hennadiy Udovenko, minister for foreign affairs of Ukraine, formulated the main

---

[1]   As of August 1997, Ukraine has 67 foreign embassies and consulates, in which over 1,000 people work. In Ukraine itself, 62 countries have embassies, there are 8 consulates, and representative offices for 10 international organizations.—Yu.S.

principles of the new Ukrainian administration's foreign policy:

> 1. Ukraine will strengthen its sovereignty and continue to build an independent state.
> 2. The question of whether Ukraine will belong to the East or West and where it will go is oversimplified and not precise. Our country will remain where it was from the very beginning. The main task for Ukraine as a historically old but politically new state is the gradual integration into European and world processes as a reliable link to the new global system of international relations.
> 3. The international policy of Ukraine will be more pragmatic and dynamic, predictable, consistent, and balanced.
> 4. Mutually advantageous cooperation with Russia and other states-members of the Commonwealth of Independent States will be intensified.
> 5. Ukraine is equally interested in the intensification of relations with the United States, Germany, Canada, states of Central and Eastern Europe, Asian states, first of all, with China, Japan, other countries of the Pacific Rim, as well as Africa, Latin America.

One of the priority directions for us is the development of versatile relations with the member states of the Commonwealth of Independent States (CIS) formed on the territory of the former USSR in December 1991. While developing intensive economic ties within the CIS, Ukraine will not participate in the attempts to institutionalize interstate bodies which could lead to the re-establishment of a supranational or confederative structure.

Within a short period of time in Leonid Kuchma's presidency relations with a number of CIS countries have intensified. Summit meetings took place with leaders of Georgia, Turkmenistan, Moldova, Kazakhstan, Lithuania, Estonia. Within the CIS framework Ukraine signed a treaty on economic cooperation but refrained from joining the Russia-dominated defense bloc and rejected Ukraine's inclusion into the system of the so-called "external borders of the CIS." Of particular importance for Ukraine are its relations with Russia. A major bilateral Treaty on Friendship and Cooperation is to be finalized and signed by Ukrainian President Leonid Kuchma and Russian President Boris Yeltsin in Kyiv. The principal provisions include the recognition of state sovereignty and territorial integrity of Ukraine and respect for existing borders. Ukraine is very much interested in this treaty which is being negotiated now both in Moscow and Kyiv. Having stopped the anti-Russian rhetoric at the diplomatic level and having agreed to compromise on some issues, our country will firmly uphold the principles of its independence. We in Ukraine are very much concerned with the aggressive slogans of Zhirinovsky, who promises to abolish Ukraine's independence as soon as he comes to power. But of no less concern are the statements of a number of respectable politicians of the Russian Establishment who advise the Russian president on policy towards Ukraine. Let me cite Mr. Sergei Karaganov, a well-known analyst and adviser to President Yeltsin who during a recent visit to Kyiv (1995) stated that Ukraine should conclude a close economic Union with Russia which would envisage:

- coordination of financial and credit policy
- establishment of a system of "tied-up currencies"
- refusal to allow the portrayal of Russia as a hostile state in the government-controlled mass media
- removal of all obstacles for human exchanges
- coordination of foreign policy

In Karaganov's opinion, this position implies the creation of a close political and economic union similar to the European Union while preserving independence of its member states. Naturally, even this "soft" scenario is connected with certain political losses for Ukraine. Needless to say that much tougher scenarios of policy towards Ukraine, including those seeking the loss of its statehood, are being considered by some Russian politicians of a more imperial bent.

Let me stress again that Ukraine has no territorial claims against any neighboring country. We strive to live in peace and friendship with our great neighbor, Russia. As I mentioned, the comprehensive Ukrainian-Russian Treaty on Friendship and Cooperation is ready for signing and we hope that President Yeltsin will come to Kyiv as soon as possible to sign it. As a result of fruitful bilateral negotiations which ended recently in Kyiv, Ukraine's $2.5 billion debt was rescheduled. This is another step in overcoming existing differences.

At the same time, we oppose any attempts to exploit the so-called "Crimean issue" for the worsening of Ukrainian-Russian relations. As you may know, on March 17, 1995 the Parliament of Ukraine decided to abolish the constitution and the presidency in the Autonomous Republic of Crimea in connection with grave violations by the Crimean authorities of the constitutional provisions of Ukraine. The Crimean issue is a domestic problem in Ukraine, since Crimea is an integral constituent part of our country. The legal status of the autonomous republic is recognized by the United States and the world community at large.

Let me now address the broader issues of Ukraine's international security and express the views of Ukrainian leadership. Considering Ukraine's current position regarding European security we proceed from several fundamental facts:

1. In 1990 Ukraine, then a Soviet republic, proclaimed its non-bloc, neutral status. This was an important and positive step, because Ukraine actually became the first country within the space of the USSR to quit the Warsaw bloc. In 1993 it did not join the Tashkent bloc of Russia and seven CIS countries and in this manner fully preserved its neutrality. The neutral status of our state is a constitutional norm, and a two-thirds majority of Parliament is needed to change it. Ukraine's neutral status, however, is not an obstacle to its participation in the North Atlantic Treaty Organization (NATO) "Partnership for Peace" (PfP) Program which today comprises 25 European countries including such neutral states as Sweden, Finland, and Austria. Incidentally, Ukraine was among the first to join the PfP Program.

2. Geographically, Ukraine is a state within the Central and Eastern European region and, by God's will, it is destined to be a bridge, a joining link between political East and West. It would be a national tragedy if Ukraine finds itself between two conflicting or warring military and political blocs. It would be a universal tragedy if Ukraine again becomes a pawn of expansionist powers.

3. The overall situation in Central and Eastern Europe cannot be considered stable. Taking into account recent developments on the territory of the former Soviet Union, the issue of NATO expansion acquires today crucial importance. We believe that NATO will further seek activation of its new role as one of the basic elements of the future all-European security system which should include all NATO countries and their "cooperative partners."

4. Ukraine does not object in principle to NATO expansion into the Central and Eastern European region, but we need the understanding that Ukraine is an integral part of that region and that our security interests are to be properly guaranteed.

5. Ukraine believes that no one has the right to deny and veto any country from seeking the most effective means of achieving its national security goals, including joining NATO.

6. In Ukraine there is concern about discussion of a possible new division of Europe into "spheres of influence" and that Ukraine may become sort of "payment" to Russia for the loss of its influence in Central Europe. We consider such a postulate to be extremely dangerous and contrary to our national interests. Let me recall the warning of President Kuchma against the erection of a new "Berlin wall" on the borders of Ukraine.

7. Ukraine is ready to discuss the conditions for establishing both a special relationship and a special partnership between Ukraine and NATO within the framework of the PfP program and the North Atlantic Cooperation Council (NACC) activities.

We also understand that national security issues are very closely connected with the economic situation. At the end of the twentieth century the might of a state can be measured not only by the number of nuclear missiles, tanks, submarines and number of troops, but, first of all, by the well-being of its people, steady economic development, amounts of currency in its banks, technological and intellectual capability.

Today Ukraine is experiencing a grave structural crisis. It is torn apart by political, socioeconomic, religious and psychological contradictions, direct outgrowths of the colonial past of Ukraine as a province of the former Soviet Empire, by breakdown of usual forms of everyday life. We need a minimum of several years to consolidate the nation for the achievement of economic prosperity of the independent Ukrainian state.

Last October Ukraine's President Leonid Kuchma announced a program of radical economic reforms for Ukraine including liberalization of prices, financial stabilization, massive privatization, and liberalization of foreign economic activities. Today we are already witnessing the first signs of financial stabilization and reduction of the inflation rate. The realization of these reforms is a prerequisite for a future prosperous and secure Ukraine.

Finally, I want to address a very important component of Ukraine's security—its relationship with the United States. Within the last four years we have witnessed a tremendous progress in bilateral relations—from difficult recognition to democratic partnership. While characterizing Ukraine's relations with the United States, I want to stress that they were far from simple. We can characterize a few important stages in their development:

1. On December 25, 1991 the United States officially recognized the independence of Ukraine. It upgraded its consulate general in Kyiv to the status of an embassy in January 1992. In May of the same year the first official visit of Ukraine's president took place when first bilateral agreements were signed and Ukraine's embassy in Washington, DC was established.

2. In 1993 a deep crisis occurred in U.S.-Ukrainian relations, connected with the presence on Ukraine's territory of the world's third largest strategic group of SS-19 and SS-24 missiles (176 missiles all in all), which were proclaimed the property of Ukraine and comprised 1,240 nuclear warheads aimed at the Western countries including the U.S. Pressure on Ukraine was intensified, with the goal of making it sign the Non-Proliferation Treaty (NPT).

3. In October 1993 Secretary of State Warren Christopher traveled to Kyiv and made clear that economic support for Ukraine on the U.S. side would not be linked to the progress on the nuclear issue.

A crucial breakthrough at this point was the January 1994 Trilateral Statement signed in Moscow by the leaders of the U.S.A., Ukraine, and Russia which provided for the removal of all nuclear weapons from Ukraine. Finally, in November 1994 Ukraine acceded to the NPT and made possible the fully successful first state visit of the Ukrainian president to the U.S.

4. Last year's state visit of President Leonid Kuchma marked a new stage

in our countries' bilateral relations. We now have a good framework for our versatile ties—the Charter of Ukrainian-American Friendship, Partnership and Cooperation which recognizes strategic importance of Ukraine for the United States and European Security. Now we are heading for a new summit, this time in Kyiv where President Clinton will travel on May 11. The advance team headed by Deputy Secretary of State Strobe Talbott recently visited Ukraine. This will not be simply a courtesy visit but, a very important event for strengthening our collaboration in many aspects, including enhancement of our national security, and strengthening of economic ties.

In this connection let me repeat the words of Secretary of State Warren Christopher in his keynote speech about the U.S. policy toward the New Independent States of the former Soviet Union delivered in March 1995 at Indiana University:

> Some states of the former Soviet Union command particular attention because of their potential to influence the future of the region. Ukraine is critical. With its size and position, juxtaposed between Russian and Central Europe, it is a linchpin of European security. An independent, non-nuclear and reforming Ukraine is also vital to the success of reform in the other New Independent States.

Let me also say a few words on our important relationship with the United States Department of Defense. The recent visit of Secretary William Perry to Ukraine testifies to the continued and strengthening relations between our two military establishments. During his visit William Perry signed over $20 million of additional U.S. aid. The practical aspects of this decision will be discussed within the framework of the joint commission on implementation and inspection of the Strategic Arms Reduction Treaty (START). Ukraine also reconfirmed that it stood for the idea of permanent extension of the Non-Proliferation Treaty.

The main focus of U.S.-Ukraine relations, however, remains the field of economics and trade. As Strobe Talbott once put it, today Ukraine is for America "a friend in need." We count on U.S. and world community assistance to overcome deep economic crisis and implement radical economic reforms. As a sign of this support, last December Ukraine received a $500 million loan from the World Bank (WB) and just recently, two weeks ago, it received an almost $2 billion package of Standby and Systematic Transformation Facility (STF) loans from the

International Monetary Fund (IMF). Besides, U.S. assistance for Ukraine in 1995 is supposed to amount to no less than U.S. $250 million. Ukraine is now the world's fourth largest recipient of U.S. foreign assistance (after Israel, Egypt, and Russia). I would like to express our deep and sincere gratitude for the crucial assistance from the U.S. Government and from the U.S. people.

Over centuries Ukraine was a province of the huge Russian and then Soviet Empires. Having no statehood, the Ukrainian people began to lose its national and cultural identity. In connection with the "Russification" which intensified dramatically during Soviet leader Leonid Brezhnev's rule, the Ukrainian nation was on the verge of loss of its native tongue, its rich folk heritage. The Chornobyl disaster has endangered the very genetic existence of its people. That is why the Ukrainian people are determined to build an independent state of their own.

History has often been cruel to Ukraine. The end of the twentieth century is not the best time for the rebirth of a state. Ukraine lost its chances in the seventeenth, eighteenth, and at the beginning of the twentieth centuries. Today history is giving us a last chance to keep up with other European states and to create a new nation based on the principles of modern civil society, democracy, tolerance, and liberalism. We have to create a prosperous state and establish new relations with other countries based on equality and mutually beneficial cooperation.

Our destiny is in our hands. We want to. We can. We will make ours a fortunate destiny!

Two

Examining the New Realities of Jewish-Ukrainian Relations*

Allow me, on behalf of the government of Ukraine, to welcome you to the Embassy of Ukraine in the United States and to wish all the seminar participants and guests a productive, objective discussion regarding the new stage in Ukrainian-Jewish relations that is taking place in a free Ukraine.

We see this seminar as one of the first in a series of major events to mark and reflect upon the fifth anniversary of Ukrainian independence. Ukraine attained independence, but not without some heavy baggage from its Russian-Tsarist imperial past. This was compounded by the heavy burdens inherited from the imperial Soviet state. Our social morals were degraded; historical amnesia was forced upon us; our national and spiritual heritage was ruined, and our international relations were tumultuous. All of this affected Ukrainian-Jewish relations, and with the assistance of professional hate-mongers, came a long period of crime and bloodshed.

Fortunately, courageous, honest, and wise individuals came forth from both the Ukrainian side and the Jewish side. These were individuals who were able to break the vicious circle of hatred, ignorance, and blindness. From these individuals flowed a Ukrainian-Jewish dialogue and a rapprochement which began at the end of the 1950s and the beginning of the 1960s in the United States, Canada, and Israel.

With respect to the specific nature of today's seminar, I would like to make several observations:

First, it seems to me that there is special significance in the fact that the seminar is being held on the territory of the United States of America, where the Jewish and Ukrainian communities are among the largest and most influential, and where these communities can work

* Transcript of a dialogue sponsored by the American Jewish Committee and the Embassy of Ukraine (Washington, DC, March 25, 1996).

through Congress and other political bodies and organizations to influence, at least to some extent, U.S. foreign policy. The development of a fruitful and tolerant dialogue between the Ukrainian and the Jewish communities in the United States is in the national interest of an independent Ukraine.

Second, in my opinion it is very important to condemn any attempts to place collective blame upon the entire Ukrainian people for the allegedly "genetic" anti-Semitism and crimes committed by the Nazis during World War II on the territory of Ukraine; just as it is important to condemn any attempts to place collective blame on the entire Jewish people for participation in Lenin's and Stalin's criminal activities and NKVD repression of the Ukrainian and other peoples.

Third, it would be desirable if the work of the seminar was directed not only at the past, with its dark as well as bright pages, but, as a first priority, at the future, which to a great extent depends on us and how we build the independent Ukranian state as a free, open, democratic society of Ukrainians, Russians, Jews, and members of other nationalities united by Ukrainian citizenship.

Let me point out one very important aspect of the policies of an independent Ukraine. I am referring to the relations between Ukraine and Israel. I had the honor of being Ukraine's first ambassador to the State of Israel, and I am proud of the fact that the development of wide-scale, bilateral ties became one of the priority directions for Ukrainian policy in the Middle East. Israel is of great significance to Ukraine because of its geographic proximity to the Black Sea and the Mediterranean Sea basins, the convenience of sea and air connections between the countries, the significant potential for mutually beneficial cooperation in the fields of economics, trade, science, and culture, as well as the presence in Israel of up to 300,000 immigrants from Ukraine.

Our relations are being built on a solid juridical foundation which consists of nearly twenty treaties and protocols between the two states and governments in the political, commercial, economic, consular and other areas. In the four years of diplomatic relations between Ukraine and Israel there have been visits by the president of Ukraine to Israel and the prime minister of Israel to Ukraine, the chairman of the Parliament of Ukraine, the speaker of the Knesset, foreign ministers of both countries, and other high officials. Trade between Ukraine and Israel is growing dynamically, from $31 million in 1993 to $90 million in 1995. Our countries have traveled the road from the bitter, implacable confrontation of Soviet times to today's present relations as partners. For example, Ukraine supports U.S. and Israeli policies on the Middle East peace process, including a resolution of the Palestinian question. I would like to remind everyone that, as enunciated by the president of Ukraine, Leonid Kuchma, Ukraine resolutely and unequivocally condemns the increased terrorist activity of the Hamas extremist organization on Israel's territory, which has led to numerous victims among Israel's civilian population. We look forward to a continued widening of Ukrainian-Israeli cooperation in all areas, including defense, as well as to the development of trilateral Ukrainian-Israeli-American cooperation in these strategic directions.

I want to conclude my brief presentation by saying that we are looking forward to more cooperation in the triangle formed by the United States, Israel, and Ukraine, and I think that the main problem confronting us is the fight against terrorism. This is of great concern to us, since we also have certain problems in this area. On the territory of Ukraine, we have 500,000 illegal aliens who want to cross the border. That has led to a worsening of the crime situation. Ukraine, with its open borders, is ripe to become a victim of terrorism. So it is very important for us to work together with Israel, which has great experience in this area, and the United States of America. And there are other projects that we would like to implement in line with this cooperation.

In my opinion, Israel, Ukraine, and the United States are connected vessels—due to the communities, the diasporas, that connect them. The U.S. has both a diaspora of Ukrainians who left Ukraine, but also a diaspora of Jews who left Ukraine. And Israel has its own diaspora of Ukrainian citizens. These are people who left Ukraine with knowledge of the Ukrainian language and Ukrainian culture and life. They lived together with us, ethnic Ukrainians, and they have had the same experiences of those who remained in Ukraine. And, in some sense, they often know more about Ukraine than many ethnic Ukrainian members of the diaspora here in the United States, who unfortunately were severed from Ukraine long ago. This is our reality. And so this circulation and communication among the diasporas can be very productive in creating a civil society and creating a national life of various minorities in all three countries. This is the model for creating a civil society, because otherwise there are conflicts which begin with nationality and language questions and then turn into permanent conflicts.

So we will have to meet again. But, as for now, provocation is a very important issue. I would like to remind you that after 1917, when the independent Ukrainian National Republic was declared, the Bolsheviks and the Cheka/NKVD fought a malicious fight against Ukrainian nationalist ideas as well as against Zionist ideas. One of my first assignments in Israel was to go over materials from the KGB archives in Ukraine concerning Zionists that were prosecuted in 1921 for opposing the labor movement in Palestine. And, of course, events in 1921 were different from what happened in the 1930s through the 1950s. The Soviets portrayed both Ukrainian nationalism and Jewish Zionism as a curse and, of course, the Second World War added more bloody pages to the history of Jewish-Ukrainian relations. All of this was used as propaganda by the Soviet government against Zionism, against Ukrainian national aspirations, and against friendly Jewish-Ukrainian relations. I was present when the Demjanjuk case was heard in Israel. One must realize that it was designed as an opportunity for provocation because we know that if the death penalty was sentenced, then the KGB was ready to add more information to the case in order to prove that he was not guilty.[1] In this way, Ukrainians and Jews would be instigated to fight for a long time. Israel would be blamed for a gross injustice, because Israel had initiated the case.

Luckily, we are in an age when people write objectively and positively about Ukraine. Of course, they also write many negative things, but the important thing is that they have started to write about the country. We would like to be treated with respect, as any normal country, and to be viewed as a normal country— not as if we were some kind of a strange nation with weapons in our hands, ready to kill everyone.

---

[1]   This information came from the Israeli lawyer who represented Demjanjuk, Yoram Sheftel. He maintained that the KGB had planned the release of documents exhonerating Demjanjuk as "Ivan the Terrible," if the Israeli trial had led to his execution. In this way, Ukrainians around the world would have been incited to speak out against the government of Israel and enmity between Ukrainians and Jews would be encouraged further.—Yu.S.

We do not pretend that we have no sins. But Dr. Gluzman said that we all need to be aware of the information, of the anti-Semitic provocation, and Dr. Finberg[2] has talked about this, as well. Let us speak the truth, let us tell the Jewish community in America the realities of what is happening in Ukraine. Unfortunately, because we do not have extensive resources, the work that the Embassy can do is limited. Therefore, it is incumbent on us to work together on this. I think that the seminar today was very worthwhile. The atmosphere it fosters is tremendously valuable. I would not want for us to simply leave what has come out of this meeting here and do nothing about it. I hope that we will take this atmosphere of cooperation and mutual understanding and apply it on a practical level.

2 Participants in the dialog. Dr. Semyon Gluzman is an internationally known psychiatrist and noted Ukrainian human rights advocate. Dr. Leonid Finberg, a sociologist and director of the Kyiv Institute for Jewish Studies, is also a human rights activist and leading figure in Kyiv's Jewish community.—editor

THREE

Chornobyl: The First Decade (A Challenge to the World Community)*

I am pleased and honored to be here with you this morning at world-famous Columbia University at a forum that is so close and special to me, having been an eyewitness of those sad events, at a conference commemorating the victims of the Chornobyl catastrophe and addressing the burning issues of how to deal with its drastic consequences.

By the totality of its consequences, the accident at the Chornobyl nuclear power plant in 1986 is the largest modern disaster, a national calamity that touched upon the destinies of millions of people living on vast territories. This catastrophe brought before the Soviet Union and the world community at large the necessity of solving new and extremely complex and comprehensive problems dealing practically with all spheres of human existence: the political and social system, the economy, industrial development and the state of science and technology, legal norms and laws, culture and morals.

In the chain of the worst technogenic disasters of the 20th century, Chornobyl occupies a special place. This is an absolutely new phenomenon of modern technical civilization that has a number of characteristics that make it unprecedented. The first peculiarity is the "peaceful" character of the catastrophe, if one could describe it that way. No one planned a military operation under the code name "Chornobyl"; there was no subversion or sabotage. Chornobyl emerged as if out of nothing, anonymously; it was forecast by no one. The catastrophe became possible due to the combination of a number of incidental factors in which, however, an ominous regularity can be seen. This regularity can be described as the threat presented by the ever-growing complexity and unreliability of technical supersystems, and the concentration and centralization of huge energy, chemical, informational and biological ca-

---

* Delivered on April 9, 1996 at the Columbia University conference "Chornobyl: Ten Years After."

pacities which can grow out of control and pose a threat to mankind's sustainable development. Chornobyl is an alarm signal sent to mankind from the future; it is a warning about the possible destruction of humankind and the environment as a result of the quite good intentions of technocrats. But, as we know, "the road to hell is paved with good intentions." Chornobyl was a hard blow to the technocratic philosophy of old optimistic rationalism. There is a world fraternity of technocrats propagating technological chauvinism and technological imperialism, that is, the idea of supremacy of the technosphere over all other areas of human spiritual activity, such as people's morality, trust in God, intuitive insight, and the ability to forecast possible consequences. Chornobyl has shown that humankind's advances in technology can lead to deleterious dead ends.

The second peculiarity of Chornobyl is its global character. A catastrophe of this scale knows no boundaries, no political, social or national barriers. The territory of Ukraine, Belarus, and Russia that was contaminated by radiation exceeding 1 curie per square kilometer totals about 145,000 square kilometers with a population of 7 million. This area is equivalent to the territory of Belgium and Austria taken together. Other countries contaminated by Chornobyl include Poland, Finland, Georgia, Sweden, Norway, Austria, Bulgaria, Hungary, Romania, Italy, Great Britain, Switzerland, Germany, Turkey, Greece, and Yugoslavia. Chornobyl has acutely raised the question of the necessity of international regulations and international cooperation in case of global disasters.

Chornobyl's third peculiarity is its destructive impact on the state, political, and economic system of the former Soviet Union. It was a stability and soundness test for all state mechanisms charged with quick decision-making on issues related to the security of millions of people and informing the population. The command and administrative one-party system of the former Soviet Union did not survive the Chornobyl test and completely lost its credibility among the people. At the same time, we have to admit that under conditions of that authoritarian and centralized system, in order to overcome the results of the catastrophe, Soviet authorities managed the existing human and material resources of this huge country and drew upon the economic, military, police, science, technology and medical potential of the USSR to effect large-scale and unprecedented measures. To overcome the catastrophe's consequences, 210 military units of chemical engineering troops and air forces were mobilized, totaling about 340,000 enlisted men. About 2,500 medical doctors and 5,000 nurses were employed; about 400 special medical units were formed. In the construction of the "shelter," the sarcophagus, 10,000 workers were employed, 360,000 tons of concrete were used, about 500,000 tons of metal constructions were erected. For the population evacuated from the zone, about 21,000 houses were built and 15,000 new apartments provided. In 1987 the construction of a new city, Slavutych, for Chornobyl nuclear power plant personnel was initiated, and the city's population is now 26,000. As a result of these unprecedented measures, the economic losses, even when calculated in very low Soviet prices, amounted to over $10 billion, and the indirect costs were $25 billion. Over recent years, the new independent Ukrainian state had to spend $800 million to $900 million per year to solve post-Chornobyl problems.

The fourth and maybe the most important peculiarity of Chornobyl is that this catastrophe existed on a national scale, thus we see the problem of the internal stability of any state having nuclear power plants, as well as the problem of protecting such facilities from hostilities or terrorism. The possibility of a civil war should be eliminated in countries where nuclear plants are located. It is easy to imagine the consequences for mankind if there were nuclear plants in Bosnia, Chechnya, Tajikistan, or other hot spots of the planet. We believe that it is high time to conclude a special international agreement that would proclaim as a crime against humanity any hostilities on the territory of countries having nuclear power plants, irrespective of the reasons or character of the conflict (whether it is an ethnic or religious one, a civil war or an invasion by a foreign country, etc.) It is also necessary to elaborate an effective mechanism for rapid reaction by U.N. forces or other international organizations in case of the initiation of armed conflict on territories where nuclear plants are located. Chornobyl's experience shows us how dangerous the destruction of a reactor is; at the time of the explosion, there were over 230 metric tons of nuclear fuel (uranium) in the reactor. According to official data, as a result of the accident over 90 million curies of radioactivity were released, though the real figures are much higher. Even now in the ruins of the fourth reactor (i.e., within the sarcophagus) 180 tons of nuclear fuel remain, including over 2.3 tons of uranium-235 and 700 kilograms of plutonium with general radioactivity of 20 million curies. I want to remind you that an atomic bomb of the Hiroshima type contained only 10 kilograms of plutonium. Any hostilities, even those using conventional arms, pose the threat of a conflict turning into a nuclear war.

The fifth peculiarity is the involvement in the catastrophe of large population masses—first of all children, the presence of thousands of environmental refugees, long-term contamination of soil and water, and irreversible changes in the natural environment and ecosystems. By mid-August of 1986, in Ukraine over 90,000 people from 81 settlements were evacuated, in Belarus—25,000 people from 107 settlements. From 1990 to 1995, due to the radiation conditions and because of social and psychological factors, 52,000 citizens of Ukraine, 106,000 citizens of Belarus, and more than 46,000 people in Russia were resettled. According to the latest data, as a result of the accident 50,500 square kilometers of Ukraine's territory, with a population of 2.4 million in 2,218 settlements, were contaminated. A dead zone has formed around the Chornobyl Nuclear Power Plant, covering an area of 2,044 square kilometers, encompassing two cities and 74 villages.

The sixth peculiarity of Chornobyl is the presence of considerable social, psychological, and medical consequences. Despite the fact that a relatively small number of people died immediately after the accident (31 persons died of acute radiation sickness, as compared to hundreds during the chemical disaster in the Indian city of Bhopal), the long-term consequences are grave and cause great tension in the work of state agencies and medical services of Ukraine. For example, 5,000 people have lost the ability to work. The sickness of 30,000 so-called "liquidators" is officially attributed to the aftermath of the catastrophe. According to Greenpeace Ukraine, over 32,000 people died as a result of the accident. The population mortality in the most affected regions increased by 15.7 percent as compared to the pre-accident period. A group of Kyiv researchers (S. Komissarenko et al., 1994) has conducted a medical survey of a group of liquidators and has found that the majority of these people have chronic fatigue syndrome accompanied by depression of a certain subclass of lymphocytes, the so-called natural killer cells. These defects of the natural immune system were named "Chornobyl AIDS"; in the short term, this could cause an increased rate in leukemias and malignant tumors, and makes a person more susceptible to "normal infections," like bronchitis, tonsillitis, pneumonia, etc., which last longer and acquire severe clinical forms. In contaminated regions of Ukraine and Belarus there was a sharp increase (by 10 times) of thyroid cancer morbidity. Chornobyl has given rise to a psychological syndrome comparable to that suffered by veterans of war in Vietnam and Afghanistan. Among children evacuated from the zone there has been a 10- to 15-fold increase in the incidence of neuro-psychiatric disorders.

Immediately after the accident, on the orders of the Communist Party, a political and propagandist battle in interpreting the possible medical consequences of Chornobyl was begun. The official representatives of Soviet medicine, as well as some representatives of the nuclear industry complex in the West, tried to deny any consequences of Chornobyl for human health. For that these people were nicknamed "Chornobyl nightingales," i.e. extreme optimists. On the other hand, there were "black pessimists" who forecast the death of nearly the entire Ukrainian nation. The truth is that the medical consequences are undoubtedly there, but taking into the account the exceptional complexity, the multitude of factors and the durability of Chornobyl's aftermath, today it is very difficult to give a final quantitative estimate. This explains huge discrepancies in data about deaths caused by the accident that are cited by authors from different organizations. At the same time, however, it is immoral to deny serious medical consequences for the health of people in Ukraine and Belarus, such as have appeared recently in some respectable Western publications. This could be compared to publications in anti-Semitic newspapers stating there were no gas chambers in Auschwitz, or no Nazi crimes at Babyn Yar.

An important seventh peculiarity of Chornobyl is that, even after 10 years, it still requires the close attention of the international community. The world at large must finally comprehend that Chornobyl is not an international affair of Ukraine. The closure of the plant means the loss of at least 7 percent of electricity produced at the same time as an acute energy shortage, as well as the possible loss of 5,000 jobs. The estimated costs of the shutdown, including the creation of new energy sources and social protection for the personnel, are $4.4 billion (U.S.). The building of a new sarcophagus will require approximately $750 million. Ukraine and the G-7 countries last December signed a formal agreement on a cooperative plan to shut down the whole Chornobyl plant by the year 2000. The agreement establishes that the European Union and the U.S.

will help Ukraine devise plans to mitigate the effects of the shutdown on local populations. It also sets up mechanisms to allow donor countries to expedite safety improvements at the reactors still in use. In addition, the agreement provides for international cooperation in decommissioning the plant, as well as in the biggest problem of all: an ecologically sound, long-term replacement for the sarcophagus that was built around the ruins of reactor No. 4.

Perhaps the most tragic peculiarity of Chornobyl is that mankind has yet to fully understand the dramatic consequences of the accident and the warnings it brings. Chornobyl must teach the nations of the world a dreadful lesson in preparedness if we are to rely on superpowerful and hyperdangerous nuclear technology. Humankind lost a sort of innocence on April 26, 1986. We entered a new post-Chornobyl era, and we have yet to realize all the consequences. May God save mankind from any new Chornobyl.[1]

---

[1]   For a further development of this topic, see Yuri M. Shcherbak, "Ten Years of the Chornobyl Era." *Scientific American* 274(4) April 1996: 32–37.—editor

Remarks at the CSIS Trilateral Meeting of the Ambassadors of Germany, Poland, and Ukraine to the United States*

Let me express my deep gratitude to the CSIS and Dr. Zbigniew Brzezinski personally for the kind invitation of myself and my colleagues, ambassadors from Germany and Poland, to discuss a very important issue for Ukraine—the establishment of closer relations among our three states and the role of this partnership in the new European security architecture.

I would like to remind you that during the two most dramatic events in the twentieth-century history of Europe—World War I and World War II—our nations were directly involved in bloody manslaughter and lost a considerable part of their populations. Furthermore, our nations experienced dramatic changes in their status and territorial integrity. They were occupied by foreign troops, which resulted in the Yalta agreements, which in turn led to more than forty years of Cold War and domination by Communist regimes in Central and Eastern Europe, including Ukraine, Poland and a part of Germany. That is why the topic of our meeting is very important for Ukraine as well as, I hope, for our partners from Poland and Germany.

Ukraine is now looking for the best and most reliable model of European security. The main objective of our policy, as proclaimed by President Kuchma last February during his working visit to the United States, is to integrate Ukraine in the future into European economic and political structures. We also want to strengthen our ties with NATO in the framework of Partnership for Peace (PfP), having a special status. Within this model we can see that closer special collaboration between Ukraine, Poland, and Germany has the potential for becoming an addi-

* Delivered at the Center for Strategic and International Studies (Washington, D.C., April 15, 1996).

tional factor of European stability and can be fruitful for all our nations. In a practical sense, there can emerge a kind of security corridor which could become a means for a very active and positive political, economic, trade, cultural, and scientific route on the map of the European continent.

Ukrainian-Polish relationships reached the level of close partnership since the establishment of full diplomatic relations in January 1992. Incidentally, Poland was the first foreign country to recognize the state independence of Ukraine. Let me share with you one personal recollection. In September 1991, immediately after proclaiming Ukrainian independence but still before the nationwide referendum, I took part, together with Foreign Minister Anatoliy Zlenko, in very confidential talks in Warsaw with Polish Foreign Minister Krzysztof Skubiszewski. We persuaded our partners to change the status of the Polish consulate general in Kyiv to the status of special mission of the Polish government. Also, we received assurances by our host that Poland would immediately recognize Ukraine as a sovereign and independent state after the positive results of the referendum. I need not remind you that at that time the Soviet Union was still in existence. We appreciated very much such a position of our Polish friends.

The years 1992–95 saw a strengthening in bilateral ties. During the official visits by the presidents of the two countries, respectively in May 1992 and in May 1993, the interstate "Treaty of Neighborhood, Friendly Relationship and Cooperation" was signed and the Consultative Committee by the Presidents of Ukraine and Poland was set up. The Committee, which comprises two working groups of experts: foreign policy and security, and national minorities, coordinates the development of cooperation in various fields, specifically, within the Partnership for Peace Program (PfP0, in the framework of the OSCE and UN. Poland actively supported Ukraine's admission to the Council of Europe and is backing Ukraine's membership in the Central-European initiative.

In 1995, the prime ministers of the two countries met twice in Warsaw. Also, the marshall of the Polish Sejm visited Ukraine at the invitation of the speaker of the Ukrainian Parliament. The Ukrainian minister of defense visited Poland in October of that year.

An important element of a new architecture of cooperation and security is transboundary ties within the international association "Carpathian Euroregion" which comprises the Carpathian regions of

Poland, Hungary, the Slovak Republic, and Ukraine. Direct ties have been established between various cities, towns, and regions of Poland and Ukraine. The Ukrainian-Polish Commission on cooperation in the field of science and technology, the Joint Committee on Environmental Protection and the Intergovernmental Coordinating Committee held their sessions in 1995–96. Quite important in bilateral cooperation is machine-building, industry, agricultural-food industry, communication, power industry, etc. Cooperation in the military field has been very productive. The joint Ukrainian-Polish battalion is now in the process of establishment, and the joint military exercises will be held.

Of particular importance is cooperation in the humanitarian field, especially taking into account that over 200,000 Poles live in Ukraine and over 350,000 Ukrainians live in Poland. Numerous public organizations of people of Ukrainian descent in Poland and citizens of Polish origin in Ukraine are very active. So far there have not been major problems on the national minority issues, which is a very good sign indeed.

Another very important factor is the growing cooperation in the trade and economic fields. For example, Poland occupies first place in the number of established joint ventures in Ukraine. Last year our bilateral trade turnover reached $1 billion. The prospects for fruitful cooperation between the two countries are very good.

Diplomatic relations between Ukraine and the Federal Republic of Germany (FRG) were established in January 1992. The FRG was among the first G-7 nations to recognize Ukraine. Since then the relationship has been on the rise. Chancellor Helmut Kohl visited Ukraine in 1993. A Joint Declaration on bilateral cooperation was signed. The visits to Ukraine by Foreign Minister Klaus Kinkel, Minister of Defense Volker Rühe and numerous other high officials took place in 1993. During this period the Ukrainian prime minister, various other ministers, and members of Parliament visited Germany. Bilateral cooperation in the military field is very intensive. In 1994–95 over twenty working meetings between the high military officials of the two countries took place.

In January 1995, a residential area for 1,696 apartments for the Ukrainian military was commissioned in Kyiv and built at FRG expense. In February last year an intergovernmental agreement to fight organized crime and terrorism was signed in Bonn. The development of inter-parliamentary ties between Ukraine and Germany has likewise been very productive. In April 1995 the speaker of the Ukrainian parliament, Oleksandr Moroz, visited the FRG at the invitation of the Bundestag's president. President Kuchma met Chancellor Kohl in Budapest in December 1994 during the OSCE Summit. A new impulse to the development of bilateral cooperation was given during President Kuchma's official visit to Germany in July 1995. Chancellor Kohl is planning to visit Ukraine this September.

Thus, a political dialogue between the two countries has been established and a legal base for further cooperation in various fields has been created. German businessman can find Ukraine attractive, in our view, by the relatively stable political situation, well-developed industry and infrastructure, and skilled labor. In October 1995 a delegation of state-secretaries (deputy-ministers) of the federal ministries of the German Government visited Ukraine to map out priorities for economic cooperation. A similar delegation from Ukraine is to visit the FRG soon. An intergovernmental Ukrainian-German Council has been in operation since March 1992. Cooperation to overcome the consequences of the Chornobyl catastrophe has also been fruitful.

An important place in the bilateral cooperation is occupied by the ties between scientific and technological institutions of both countries, specifically the National Academy of Sciences, and space agencies. Mutually advantageous ties have been developed in culture and education. Partnership relations between towns, cities, and regions of our countries flourish.

The FRG renders considerable assistance to Ukraine in its relations with European Union, NATO, Council of Europe and international financial organizations.

We hope there are good preconditions for the beginning of a process of preliminary talks (maybe on the expert level in Kyiv, Warsaw, or Bonn) for the establishment of the European security corridor. Our three countries could constitute the first element of this. The main directions of such cooperation, as we see it, could be:

- regular official and working meetings of the three states' leaders; the candid exchange of political information
- regular political consultations and contacts among the three ministries of foreign affairs on urgent issues of European and

world life. Among the first steps along this line could be the preparation of a joint article by the three ministers on the topic of European security

- cooperation in the field of coal mining and modernization of energy-producing facilities
- adoption of the trilateral agreement on transport communication (both automobile and railroads)
- cooperation in development of modern communication systems
- elaboration of the trilateral concept of jointly combating organized crime and terrorism
- coordination and cooperation in customs, especially regarding the prevention of illegal drugs, arms, fissionable materials traffic, as well as prevention of the illegal movement through Poland to Ukraine of cars stolen in Germany
- establishment of the customs Berlin-Katowice-Lviv-Kyiv corridor which would be standardized according to European norms with a unified customs procedures, especially on prevention of illegal drugs, arms, fissionable materials trafficking, etc.
- enhanced cooperation of border troops, law enforcement bodies in combating and prevention of illegal migration. (This is a very important issue because right now on the territory of Ukraine there are about 500,000 illegal migrants from such countries as Vietnam, Tajikistan, China, and Afghanistan, whose main goal is to reach Poland, Germany and other developed European countries)
- there are plans to open two transportation corridors—a Berlin-Kyiv highway with the cost of ECU 1.4 billion, as well as Gdansk-Odesa transportation corridor, 1816 km long and costing ECU 2.2 billion
- a very interesting option is the creation of the Ukrainian-Polish-German center for technology exchange and transfer, including the conclusion of contracts for the use of Ukrainian missiles "Zenith" and "Cyclone" for space exploration, as well as serial production of the AN-70 aircraft, etc.
- the National Bank of Ukraine is ready to develop cooperation and exchange of experience in the banking sphere and currency control (as you may know, the banking system in Ukraine is developing along the German model)
- last but not least, the Ministry of Environmental Protection and Nuclear Safety is looking forward to the trilateral collaboration in

the field of ecology and reactor safety, study and overcoming the consequences of the Chornobyl accident.

Fully realizing current differences among the three countries, we at the same time believe that the creation of a proposed partnership pattern between Germany, Poland, and Ukraine—states belonging to different regions of Europe—would contribute to the strengthening of security and the establishment of a kind of "stability belt" in a part of Europe that over centuries has been characterized by instability and even mutual hostility. We are convinced that the development of regional cooperation according to the formula "Europe of regions" will be an important part of the German and Polish concept of continual integration of which Ukraine wants to be a part, given our common industrial potential and the 165 million people living in our countries that are linked not only by geography but also by history and destiny.

FIVE

Marked by Unprecedented Vitality: On the Fifth Anniversary of the Establishment of Diplomatic Relations between Ukraine and the United States*

The relationship between independent Ukraine and the United States, despite its relatively short time-span, is marked by unprecedented vitality and packed with important events of significance both for Europe and the world at large. It testifies to the constructiveness of the approach adopted by both sides in their desire to solve problems as well as to the growing mutual understanding and interactions between them.

To sum up the process of establishing and developing Ukrainian-American state relations for the past five years one can define certain stages, "ebbs and tides," each of which reflects the peculiarities of domestic political climate in Ukraine and in the United States, their international status and the situation in the world.

The Winding Road to Recognition

President Bush's speech at the Supreme Soviet of the UkrSSR in Kyiv on August 1, 1991 (it was ironically called "Chicken Kiev" by the press at that time) could be counted as the zero (if not below zero) point of the starting point of our relations. In this speech the American president said, "Freedom is not the same thing as independence. Americans will not support those who gain independence in order to trade a distant tyranny for local despotism. Americans will not help those who stand for suicidal nationalism and ethnic hatred." In her stimulating 1995 master's thesis (Naval Postgraduate School) "From Chicken Kiev to Ukrainian Recognition" Susan Fink claims that Mykhail Gorbachev

---

* Originally published in Ukrainian in *Politika i chas* 1996 (11): 3–17 as "Poznacheni bezpretsedentnym dynamizmom." Translated by Volodymyr Dibrova.

tried to talk President Bush out of going to Kyiv, fearing that the American president's visit could encourage "Ukrainian nationalists." Yet President Bush did venture to visit the capital of Ukraine, but before going there—and this is something that has no precedent in the history of a superpower like the United States—he showed the text of his speech to the Secretary General of the Communist Party of the Soviet Union and strengthened the pro-Union, pro-Gorbachev emphasis in it. Bush's speech in Kyiv was immediately criticized by Senator Dennis DeConcini (D-AZ) and caused an outcry among Ukrainian-Americans.

During the period between the Declaration of State Independence on August 24, 1991 and the national referendum on December 1, 1991, when Ukraine was *de jure* a part of the USSR, the United States underwent a difficult and painful process of reassessing and changing its foreign policy directions. On the one hand, the traditional "Moscow-centric" tendency, expressed mainly by the U.S. Department of State remained strong and almost intact. American foreign policy makers advocated the preservation of a Soviet Union, somewhat liberalized by "perestroika" and "glasnost," because they seemed to believe that the emergence on the territory of the former USSR of a number of new nation-states armed with nuclear weapons could create a complicated and highly confusing situation that would run counter to U.S. interests in the region.

The dangerous illusions as to the ability of Gorbachev to consolidate the nation, whose breakup became a *fait accompli,* bespoke a fatal misunderstanding (on the part of some U.S. governmental agencies and politicians) of the profound processes under way in Ukraine and other republics of the USSR as well as their underestimation of the strength of the national-liberation movement and the general disillusionment with Moscow and Gorbachev.

On the other hand, a number of sober-minded politicians (and one cannot help mentioning an outstanding role played by then Defense Secretary Richard Cheney) realized the necessity of recognizing the independence of Ukraine and establishing full diplomatic and state relations between the United States and Ukraine.

The U.S. Congress and the Ukrainian-American community contributed a great deal to the changes in American policy towards Ukraine. Under constant pressure from the Ukrainian lobby on November 20, 1991 the U.S. Senate passed a resolution urging President Bush to recognize Ukraine. On November 29, 1991 on the eve of the referendum in Ukraine, President Bush met fifteen representatives of Ukrainian-American organizations in the United States, who on behalf of the Ukrainian-American constituency voiced their opinion that it was independent Ukraine and not Gorbachev's Soviet Union that was vitally important to U.S. national interests. Equally important were the pre-election maneuvers of the Democratic Party, that by unequivocally supporting Ukrainian independence seized the initiative from Bush. The pivotal importance of Ukrainian-American votes in the election cannot be ruled out.

On December 25, 1991, on the seventeenth day after the historic Bilovezhsk decisions, on the third day after the CIS leaders meeting in Almaty, and right after Gorbachev's resignation—when it became absolutely clear that the USSR had politically and legally seized to exist—the United States of America officially recognized independent Ukraine. Diplomatic relations between them were established on January 23, 1992. The fact that the United States had already had a consulate general in Kyiv, headed by John Gunderson, considerably facilitated the problem of strengthening bilateral contacts and created the basis for opening a full-fledged American diplomatic presence in Ukraine.

The Crisis of Confidence

In 1992–1993 bilateral relations between Ukraine and the United States were carried on in an atmosphere of distrust and suspicion, created by the American administration and media which tended to view Ukraine in a fairly unfavorable light.

The appearance of a new world player—independent Ukraine—on whose territory the world's third largest stock of strategic nuclear weapons was amassed and aimed at the West prompted mixed feelings in the United States and some European countries. Feelings ranged from extreme pessimism—apprehension and premonition that events might take a turn for something completely unpredictable and could possibly destabilize this strategically important region—to optimistic hope that the new-born nation-state would opt for democracy.

It should be mentioned that for a certain period of time right after the breakup of the Soviet Union the cumbersome mechanism of the U.S. government in its foreign policy continued to follow the old well-trodden path, which was dominated by a traditional bipolar approach. That is, despite the emergence on the territory of the former USSR of new independent states with different, and sometimes opposing, national interests, the United States recognized Russia as the sole legal heir to the USSR and tried to act according to a "Russia above all" doctrine, giving Russia a priority status and singling it out as the chief U.S. rival and partner.

In a 1994 article in the journal *Politychna dumka/Political Thought* (Kyiv) the prominent American analyst Sherman Garnett quite aptly remarked that:

> The West is still unaccustomed to dealing with the territory of the former USSR as a region of international diplomacy. At least a partial reason for this reluctance lies with the West's reliance in a time of change on strategic continuities that would guide its policies, even as they delayed engagement with new realities. The two most important continuities are its continued support for reforms in Moscow and its focus on nuclear weapons, particularly the problem of a nuclear Ukraine ("The Ukrainian Question and the Future of Russia," *Politychna dumka/Political Thought* 94[4]: 169–70).

Some U.S. politicians refused to accept the new reality and continued to consider Ukraine an integral part of Russia. Expressing this line of thinking, Jerry F. Hough wrote in *The New York Times* in 1993:

> The Soviet superpower may be gone, but Russia and Ukraine still have nuclear weapons. It would be a disaster if Russian and Ukrainian politics evolve as politics did in Serbia and Croatia. It would be easy for Mr. Yeltsin to adopt a policy of annexing Russian-populated lands in adjoining republics in an attempt to bolster his faltering domestic support.

> Russian and Ukrainian economic integration, including a common currency and a subsidy policy coordinated with the other republics, is necessary for reform in both countries. The U.S. goal should be the loose union we support in Western Europe.

> In trying to achieve our goals, we must strive for the achievable, not the utopian, as is often the case. We should not oppose integration [of Russia and Ukraine—Yu. S.] and insist on full economic and military independence of Ukraine. If there were a crisis in Russian-Ukrainian relations and we, siding with Ukraine, imposed economic and technological sanctions on Russia, the Russian Army would support Serbia-style annexation.

> But the Russian Army and leaders of defense industry managers are our natural allies ("Russia Aims its Oil Weapon," *New York Times* 17 June 1993: A25).

During this difficult period the main task of Ukrainian foreign policy vis-à-vis the United States was to get from it a meaningful recognition of Ukraine as an equal partner, as a nation that occupies an important geopolitical position in Europe and has its own interests that could differ from those of neighboring post-Soviet countries. In other words, we had to prove that we could be a bona fide nation-state, could have our own state institutions, and conduct an effective independent foreign policy. The advanced group in charge of setting up the Ukrainian Embassy in Washington, DC was formed in February 1992 and consisted of Serhiy V. Kulyk and Igor I. Dunaiskyi. On March 6, 1992 a presidential decree appointed Oleh H. Bilorus to be the first Ukrainian ambassador to the United States. On May 5, 1992 he presented his credentials to President Bush. On July 9, 1992 the first U.S. ambassador to Ukraine Roman Popadiuk, an American of Ukrainian descent, presented his credentials to the Ukrainian president.

The first official working visit of President Leonid Kravchuk to the United States took place on May 5–11, 1992. During his meetings with President Bush, Secretary of State James Baker, Defense Secretary Cheney and other officials a number of important documents were signed, among them a political declaration, a memorandum on mutual understanding between the governments of Ukraine and United States, agreements on trade relations, on environmental protection, on encouragement of capital investments, on humanitarian, scientific, technical cooperation and others. I had the honor of being a member of the Ukrainian delegation, signing one of the first Ukrainian-American agreements and experiencing the sheer, unforgettable exhilaration brought about by the realization of the historic significance of the event. It is noteworthy that Leonid Kuchma, a member of the delegation and an MP, was the only one whom Americans allowed to examine the space-shuttle at the Johnson Space Center in Houston, Texas.

However, despite the term "democratic partnership" between Ukraine and the United States present in the political declaration, any sort of "honeymoon" in Ukrainian-American relations had to be put off until later. The biggest confrontational issue of that period was the problem of Ukraine acquiring non-nuclear status. Driven by their strategic interests, which were not identical but occasionally overlapped, the United States and Russia applied additional pressure on Ukraine to make it relinquish its arsenals of tactical and strategic nuclear weapons. It was the first time that Ukrainian officials and diplomats faced such tough and consistent pressure from the world's two nuclear super-powers.

In 1992–1993 the U.S. media published a series of biased and bla-tantly anti-Ukrainian articles, often inspired by foreign propaganda centers whose purpose was to discredit Ukraine. These articles treated Ukraine with scorn and did not try to disguise their rejection of the very idea of an independent Ukraine. At the same time if one disregards the excessive "sound and fury" of the anti-Ukrainian propaganda, one can see that the criticism had two primary foci:

- Ukrainian nuclear disarmament (or refusal thereof)
- The absence of tangible economic reforms, the preservation of certain features of the Communist-Soviet regime in Ukraine

The dramatic and lively diplomatic battles connected with the issue of Ukrainian nuclear disarmament call for a separate study and are not the topic of this article. I would only like to mention that up to mid-1993 Washington assumed a tough, almost ultimatum-like position towards Ukraine. The U.S. refused to conduct a dialog on the basis of equality or to develop economic cooperation until Ukraine would ratify the START-1 and join the Nuclear Non-Proliferation Treaty (NPT). One has only to bring back the typical newspapers' and press agencies' head-lines of that time to understand the urgency of the "Ukrainian nuclear issue": "How close is Ukraine to becoming a nuclear power?," "Russia claims that Ukraine refuses to discard its nuclear weapons," "U.S. posi-tion pushes Ukraine to declare itself a nuclear power," "The West insists on Ukrainian nuclear disarmament," "A new Munich?," "A new dead-end street in world politics," "The West treats Ukraine as a 'naughty republic'," "A split on the nuclear issue in Ukraine," "U.S. Ambassador to Ukraine scares Ukraine," "Ukraine is not bargaining anything."

Today we can proudly say that Ukrainian diplomacy, although in its youth, withstood that American and Russian "Sturm und Drang," wisely played the "nuclear card" and received the best possible political advantage from its "denuclearization." After somewhat romantically declaring its intention to become a non-nuclear country in 1991, Ukraine in 1992–1994 had to work out its practical nuclear policy and nuclear diplomacy under dire domestic straits and heavy international pressure.

And one of the biggest political achievements of that period is that the Ukrainian government and Parliament managed to find the only possible strategic line, to achieve the balance of power that took into account various conflicting political interests and, above all, to present well-defined conditions for Ukrainian nuclear disarmament:

- Obtaining from the nuclear powers, United States and Russia in the first place, valid guarantees of Ukrainian national security
- Obtaining adequate financial and technical assistance from the United States, Russia as well as other countries in order to help Ukraine cope with dismantling its strategic offensive weapons
- Compensating Ukraine for tactical and strategic nuclear weapons (highly enriched uranium and plutonium) that were to be shipped from Ukraine to Russia for further disassembling

This was the strategic aim of all Ukrainian foreign policy-makers, including the Ukrainian Embassy in the United States.

Future historians of this period should pay attention to a major breakthrough—the signing by Ukraine of the Protocol to START-1 (Lisbon, May 23, 1992), which in effect turned Ukraine from the object of the Treaty to its legitimate subject. As a result, Ukraine achieved the same status as the United States and Russia.

In the fall of 1992 the new American Administration faced a dilemma: either to follow the old hopeless path of pressing Ukraine and ignoring the interests of the national security of a newly-born European country, or, without abandoning the strategic slogan "Russia above all," to shift the accents and reevaluate the geopolitical role of independent Ukraine. And to the credit of Bill Clinton's foreign policy team—Warren Christopher, Strobe Talbott, Nicholas Burns, James Collins and others—the Administration was able to quickly streamline its "Ukrainian policy," which resulted in the eventual settling of the "nuclear crisis."

The Thaw

In March 1993 *The Washington Post,* covering Ukrainian Foreign Minister Anatoliy Zlenko's official visit to the United States, singled out a number of problems that had a negative effect on the speed of Ukrainian nuclear disarmament:

- growing concern about Russia's future
- insufficient security guarantees for Ukraine from the United States
- insufficient American financial assistance for dismantling, destroying, and cleaning the environment of Ukraine-based nuclear weapons
- the absence of an agreement with Russia on the Ukrainian share of funds to be obtained from the United States and others through sale of highly enriched uranium contained in the nuclear warheads in Ukraine

On the next day the same newspaper expressed the opinion that it was only all-embracing political treaties that could persuade the Ukrainian leadership that a non-nuclear status would guarantee Ukraine's security much better than declaring itself a nuclear power.

The first gesture of reconciliation and a very important landmark in the history of U.S.-Ukrainian relations was the arrival in Kyiv at the beginning of May 1993 of Strobe Talbott, special ambassador and advisor to the secretary of state, a personal friend of President Clinton, and one of the masterminds of the United States policies toward Russia as well as toward Ukraine. In an interview in the newspaper *Holos Ukraïny* on May 11, 1993 Talbott made a very significant statement:

> The fact that we came to Kyiv first could be explained by the utmost importance that the American Administration attaches to U.S.-Ukrainian relations…By making Kyiv our first stop we stress the significance of our relations with Ukraine…I would like to confirm that not only the White House but the whole Administration has drastically overhauled our policy and relations with Ukraine. The leading U.S. government agencies participated in this work…The word "pressure" will not be used by the American delegation during these talks…The United States is not going to make Ukraine do anything that would run counter to its interests. On the contrary, the United States wants to conduct a dialog with Ukraine…We will try to talk about the nuclear weapons that remain on Ukrainian soil in a much broader context—a context that would take into account the absolutely legitimate Ukrainian demands as to its security…Besides, we shall be talking about different parameters of the notion of "security," since it is not a strictly military term. Security, as well as independence and sovereignty has an economic dimension to it. That is why we wish to talk about matters that constitute Ukrainian economic security and discuss the Ukrainian desire to be a part of European and world community.

During a visit of Ukrainian Defense Minister Kostiantyn P. Morozov to the United States in July 1993, a number of documents were signed, among them a memorandum of understanding and cooperation in defense and military contacts as well as an agreement on aiding Ukraine in dismantling its nuclear weapons, the basis of which is the Nunn-Lugar Act that provides for a $350 million of U.S. aid to Ukraine in helping it get rid of the nuclear arms and implementing the conversion program.

July 1993 saw the appointment of a new U.S. ambassador to Ukraine, William Green Miller, who on October 20, 1993 presented his credentials to Ukrainian President.

Of utmost importance for the improvement of Ukrainian-American relations were the consultations held on January 2–7, 1994 in Washington, D.C. between American officials and the Ukrainian delegation headed by Vice Prime-Minister Valeriy M. Shmarov and Deputy Minister of Foreign Affairs Borys I. Tarasiuk. During these meetings the Ukrainians talked with President Clinton, National Security Advisor Anthony Lake and Deputy Defense Secretary William Perry. It is at these trilateral talks, attended also by Russian Deputy Foreign Minister Georgiy Mamedov, that the principal parameters of the Trilateral Statement that the Ukrainian, U.S., and Russian Presidents signed on January 14, 1994 in Moscow, were agreed upon. That was a true breakthrough within the complicated trilateral relations of Ukraine, the United States, and Russia. The signing of the Trilateral Statement was preceded by a short visit by President Clinton to Ukraine, the so called "Borispil landing," that at the time acquired acute political significance. The Trilateral statement had a historic clause which proclaimed that "the United States and Russia are ready to assure Ukrainian security" provided Ukraine joins START-1 and the NPT. It is highly telling that right after the signing of the Trilateral Statement in late January 1994 Ukrainian Minister of Economy Roman V. Shpek visited Washington and brought home agreements that promised a sizable increase in American financial and economic aid.

On November 18, 1993 the Ukrainian Parliament ratified START-1 but added a number of reservations aimed at securing Ukrainian national interests. When Ukrainian conditions were met after the Trilateral Statement, the Parliament lifted the reservations and authorized the Government to exchange the ratification documents. That was a remarkable step forward in the non-proliferation of nuclear weapons, a step that eventually lead to a total "denuclearization" of Ukraine in June 1996.

The "Year of Ukraine"

With Vice-President Al Gore's blessing, the year 1994, following on the heels of the "Russian" year 1993, was called "the year of Ukraine." This was a unique year, considering the political changes in Ukraine—the election of a new Parliament and a new president, Leonid D. Kuchma—as well as the "epiphany" of the American Administration, which began to see the strategically stabilizing role of Ukraine in a volatile post-Cold War environment fraught with local and regional conflicts.

A lot of credit for this "epiphany" must go to such knowledgeable and influential U.S. politicians and policy makers as former National Security Advisor Zbigniew Brzezinski and former Secretary of State Henry Kissinger. It is not a coincidence that both of them agreed to join the Ukrainian-American Advisory Committee, a non-governmental consultative body comprised of prominent political figures from Ukraine and the United States.

In 1993 Zbigniew Brzezinski gave a clear formula of the significance of Ukrainian independence:

> Independent Ukraine changes the whole geopolitical map of Europe. Its appearance is one of the three major geopolitical events of the twentieth century. The first is the 1918 breakup of the Austro-Hungarian Empire. The second—the 1945 division of Europe into two blocs. The emergence of independent Ukraine could be considered the third event because it marks the end of Imperial Russia. And it is a lot more than the end of the Communist USSR, this is the end of the last European Empire. By breaking Imperial Russia independent Ukraine created the possibility for Russia itself—as a state and a nation—to finally become a democratic European country. So for Russia Ukrainian independence is a beneficial factor. And it is not anti-Russian. On the contrary, it is definitely pro-Russian. Because to preserve the Russian Empire its people have to live in a poor, dictatorial state. The birth of an independent Ukraine is, in other words, not only an important geopolitical but also a political and philosophical event. There were times when some of us thought that America had to make a choice between Russia and Ukraine, but now it looks as if everybody understands that good relations with both country will only strengthen European stability (*Ukraïns'ke slovo* 20 January 1993).

Henry Kissinger, pursuing the same geopolitical line, warned in 1994 that "...it is a vital American interest to see to it that Eurasia not be controlled by a single power center. In essence, we have fought two wars over this issue" (*New Perspectives Quarterly* 2[3] Summer 1994: 43).

In Washington, which is highly uncommon for this city, "the year of Ukraine" was marked by two visits—an official visit and a state one—of the Ukrainian president. Although during President Leonid M. Kravchuk's visit on March 3–7, 1994 a number of international agreements were signed, the United States expressed its desire to conclude such fundamental documents as the Charter of Ukrainian-American Partnership, Friendship, and Cooperation, only pending Ukraine's joining the Non-Proliferation Treaty. The U.S. Administration was tough in conditioning the progress in bilateral relations and future American assistance upon economic and political reforms in Ukraine. Americans believed that reforms in Ukraine were insufficient and preferred to wait and see what the outcome of the forthcoming presidential elections would be.

Kuchma's victory was enthusiastically welcomed in the United States because the political and economic views of the newly elected President gave reason to believe that the catastrophic situation in Ukraine could radically change for the better. This hope was expressed by a well-known Republican political activist of Ukrainian descent Ms. Paula Dobriansky, who wrote in *The Washington Times*:

> Fortunately, the situation in Ukraine is critical, but not hopeless. Leonid Kuchma, as the new president of Ukraine, has a unique opportunity to discard Mr. Kravchuk's flawed policies and to adopt a strategic vision capable of inspiring the nation. That vision must be of a Ukraine that is a key Central European nation and an important stakeholder in Western economic and security systems, and at the same time enjoys a constructive relationship with Russia.
>
> To realize this vision, the Ukrainian leadership must devise a comprehensive economic reform package and attract foreign investment; undertake legal and electoral changes that will break the near monopoly on power at the local and regional levels of the old nomenklatura, while enhancing the legitimacy of Ukrainian democrats; and pursue firm but sensitive Ukrainization policies that foster national identity without promoting ethnic and religious schisms. With the right set of policies, informed by sound vision, Ukraine can not only survive but flourish.

An intelligent U.S. policy could bolster these prospects. The United
States must continue to make it clear, publicly and privately, the
importance we attach to Ukraine being not only a prosperous
democracy but a sovereign and independent state with inviolable
borders (28 August 1994: B4).

At the beginning of August 1994, soon after the inauguration of
Ukrainian President Kuchma, Vice-President Gore paid an official visit
to Kyiv. There he expressed the desire to "further develop strong, large-
scale bilateral relations with Ukraine" and asked President Kuchma
to visit Washington. Gore stressed that "there is no alternative to
radical economic reforms in Ukraine." Kuchma's state visit to the
United States (November 19–23, 1994) was a turning point in the history of Ukrainian-American relations and it began a new period of interstate cooperation. The basic political document of this new era in our
relations was the Charter of Ukrainian-American Partnership, Friendship and Cooperation, signed in the White House on November 22,
1994 by Presidents Kuchma and Clinton. The parties stated that "the
existence of a free, independent and sovereign Ukrainian state, its security and prosperity is very important for the United States of America."
Ukraine and the United States "expressed their determination to build a
broad and durable partnership" and agreed that the "independence,
sovereignty and territorial integrity of the Ukrainian state are fundamental to their partnership." Both countries expressed within the Charter their understanding of the fact that:

> …Ukraine's strategic location in the center of Europe enables it to
> make a special contribution to the peace, security and stability of the
> region. Convinced that Ukraine cannot be secure until Europe as a
> whole is secure, the United States of America supports Ukrainian
> efforts to resolve differences with its neighbors in a peaceful and
> cooperative spirit, refraining from the threat or use of force against the
> territorial integrity or political independence of any other state.

The United States greeted the Ukrainian decision to participate in
NATO's "Partnership for Peace" program (PfP) and expressed its desire
to develop mutually advantageous military cooperation and to have
regular consultations on issues of international security. Especially important is a clause in the Charter, according to which:

> If in the future, an external threat to the territorial integrity, political
> independence or security of Ukraine should arise, the United States of

> America and Ukraine intend to consult and to undertake steps as appropriate to achieve a peaceful resolution consistent with international law and principles of the CSCE.

Ukraine promised to implement market-oriented reforms in the shortest possible time, and the United States of America confirmed its readiness to provide financial and political support to Ukraine both at the bilateral level as well as through international financial institutions.

The significance of the Charter is hard to overestimate: as time goes by this document only grows in stature. And everyone interested in Ukrainian-American relations should read and study it carefully.

Politically, 1994 ended on a triumphant note at the Budapest Summit of the OSCE (December 5–6, 1994) when Ukraine, in exchange for its ratification of START-1 and joining NPT, received guarantees of its national security in the form of a Memorandum—an extraordinary international law document, signed by the leaders of the United States, Great Britain, and Russia. On the same day, Ukraine received unilateral guarantees of its security from France and China. It was also confirmed that major world powers vowed to respect the independence, sovereignty, and the existing borders of Ukraine, to restrain from the threat of force or economic pressure. Whatever the skeptics have to say about the lack of guarantees (the English version of the text uses the word "assurances"), it was an unprecedented step forward. Never before, neither during the period of the Ukrainian National Republic, nor during the existence of the Ukrainian S.S.R.—let alone in the seventeenth-century during Bohdan Khmelnytskyi's Cossack state—was Ukraine a subject of such global agreement nor did it receive such universal political guarantees for its very existence.

One must acknowledge the prominent role played by the United States, which undoubtedly acted according to its national interests when it persistently and resolutely demanded the removal of offensive nuclear forces from the territory of Ukraine. Ukraine also made the only reasonable move by surrendering the nuclear weapons it was unable to maintain or effectively deploy. Having done so, Ukraine ceased to be a nuclear target for the United States and a nuclear hostage of other countries, thus securing its future from being sucked into an unexpected foreign nuclear confrontation. The road to a non-nuclear status for Ukraine was long and painful, it stretched from Lisbon via Washington and Moscow to Budapest, and on this road Ukraine gained substantial international respect, clearing up loads of debris that blocked path toward the development of a profound partnership with the United States.

Facets of Democratic Partnership

Ukrainian-American relations are being carried out in several directions:

Political contacts: It would be difficult to find countries other than Ukraine and the United States that conduct such an intensive political dialog at the level of their highest officials. The period of 1992–1996 saw five Ukrainian presidential visits to the United States (including President Kuchma's attendance of the UN 50th anniversary celebrations, where he met with President Clinton), two visits of President Clinton to Kyiv, and one visit of Vice-President Gore to Ukraine. Secretary of State Warren Christopher visited Kyiv three times and Deputy Secretary of State Strobe Talbott—five times. Since 1994 Ukrainian Foreign Minister Hennadiy Yo. Udovenko has been to the United States four times and in 1996 alone six times had the occasion to meet and talk with Secretary of State Christopher. There were seven visits of the Ukrainian minister of defense to the United States and six visits of the U.S. secretary of defense to Ukraine. The reciprocal visits of U.S. National Security Advisor Anthony Lake and his Ukrainian counterpart Volodymyr P. Horbulin were equally productive. Speakers of the Ukrainian Parliament Ivan S. Pliushch and Oleksandr O. Moroz twice visited the United States and many high ranking U.S. Congressmen were their guests in Kyiv. There were two working visits of Ukrainian prime ministers to the United States: Yevhen K. Marchuk visited in September 1995 and Pavlo I. Lazarenko—in July 1996. The latter came to Washington only fifteen days after his appointment as prime minister and visited the International Monetary Fund, the World Bank, and had meetings with prominent members of the Administration and the U.S. Congress. Regular contacts have been established between the National Bank (Viktor A. Yushchenko), Agency of Reconstruction and Development of Ukraine (Roman V. Shpek), National Property Fund (Yuriy I. Yekhanurov), and corresponding American officials (Secretary of the Treasury Robert Rubin, Special Advisor to the President of the United States Richard Morningstar, and others). Each year dozens of Ukrainian governmental and parliamentary delegations visit the United States.

Of great importance here were President Clinton's state visit to Kyiv (May 11–12, 1995), which led *The Washington Post* to call that period "a honeymoon" in U.S.-Ukrainian relations, on the eve of the working visit of President Kuchma to Washington (February 20–22, 1996). These visits raised the Ukrainian-American relations to a high level of democratic partnership.

It goes without saying that it is the quality, not the quantity of political contacts that matters most, and two recent years saw a great degree of openness, mutual understanding, trust, similarity or closeness of opinions on a number of international problems.

Among the issues discussed during the above-mentioned meetings were market reforms in Ukraine and the role of the West—the G7 countries in particular—in providing Ukraine with substantial financial and technical aid, especially for decommissioning the Chernobyl nuclear plant. The talks also dealt with Ukrainian national security in the context of building up a reliable system of European security, possible NATO expansion as well as other issues of bilateral relations. The Joint Statement of the American and Ukrainian Presidents signed in Kyiv on May 11, 1995 underscores the fact that the United States supports democratic and market-oriented reforms in Ukraine, its political sovereignty, its territorial borders and are in favor of Ukrainian desire to join European and world community. The very fact of such a statement is in itself highly unusual for American governmental practice.

A potent political signal was sent by Secretary of State Christopher during his Kyiv visit in March 1996 when, referring to a Russian Duma resolution to cancel the Belovezhsk Agreements, he said:

> One of the central issues in the future of Europe will be Russia's relationship with its newly independent neighbors. Last week, we were confronted with a dark vision of that future when the Russian Duma voted in favor of reconstituting the USSR. But history must not be reversed. Five years ago, millions of former Soviet citizens freely chose independence and the United States will continue to support their right and determination to keep it.

A Joint Ukrainian-American intergovernmental committee headed by President Kuchma and Vice-President Gore is to become a brand new element of interaction between our two countries. The committee consists of a number of subdivisions that cover a broad scope of cooperational issues in the sphere of economics, energy resources, foreign policy and the national security of Ukraine and the United States.

The *legal basis of Ukrainian-American relations* is rather impressive and consists at the moment of approximately sixty signed or ready-to-be-signed agreements and other documents. The most fruitful visit to the United States turned out to be President Kuchma's because his talks resulted in fourteen signed or declared bilateral documents. Ukrainian-American agreements opened the way to a large-scale mutually beneficial and equal partnership in political, economic, trade, scientific, technological, space, military, humanitarian and other spheres.

Financial-economic aid to Ukraine has been carried out along several channels

> 1. Assistance in the form of grants confirmed annually by the U.S. Congress and distributed by the United States Agency for International Development (USAID).
>
> 2. Credits of the Import-Export Bank of the United States.
>
> 3. Credit support from the International Monetary Fund (IMF) with the help of the United States and other countries to cover the budgetary deficit of Ukraine.
>
> 4. Preferential credits for structural reforms and designated investment projects provided by the World Bank and supported by the United States.
>
> 5. Preferential credits (PL-480) of the United States Department of Agriculture for the purchase of agricultural products (soy).
>
> 6. A program of reducing of nuclear threat (as envisaged by the Nunn-Lugar Act) carried out by the U.S. Defense Department.
>
> 7. A program of industrial partnership and securing the safety of nuclear power stations, provided by the United States Department of Energy and the Nuclear Regulatory Commission.
>
> 8. Humanitarian aid provided by different U.S. non-governmental organizations like the Children of Chornobyl Fund, the United States-Ukraine Foundation, and others.

An important, though little-known, element of the U.S. financial-economic aid to Ukraine is the assistance of the G7 countries that was initiated and sponsored by the United States. The issue of aid to Ukraine was discussed at the recent G7 summits in Naples (1994), Halifax (1995), and Moscow (1996), and had to do both with the closure of Chornobyl power plant and with a much broader economic context. Thus, the resolution of the Halifax summit stated (pt. 46):

> We welcome the good start Ukraine has made on its bold program of economic reform... We encourage Ukraine to continue its reform efforts in close cooperation with the international financial institutions. Assuming the continuation of strong economic reform, an additional $2 billion in commitments could be available from the international financial institutions by the end of 1996 (*U.S. Department of State Dispatch Supplement* 6[4] July 1995: 9).

According to official U.S. statistics U.S. budgetary aid to Ukraine in 1992–1996 provided in accordance with the Support of Freedom Act, the Program of reducing nuclear threat (Nunn-Lugar Act) and other programs reached 1.182 billion dollars U.S., 608.8 million dollars of which (51.3%) has already been spent. This compares to Russia, which received 4.112 billion dollars and has spent 2.6 billion (64%), Armenia—612.4 million dollars and spent 500.6 million (81.7%), Georgia—420.1 million dollars and spent 377.7 million (89.9%).

It should be noted that the promised 1994 programs of American aid were very quickly frozen, but during President Kuchma's November 1994 state visit to the United States the U.S. Government confirmed in writing its previous promises provided Ukraine would carry out economic reform. In May 1995 on the eve of President Clinton's state visit to Ukraine the U.S. Import-Export Bank released its 500 million dollars credit programs that were frozen in 1993 because of the worsening of Ukrainian financial situation and overdue Ukrainian national and commercial debts to the United States. Beginning in 1995, in accordance with the Joint Act of the House of Representatives and the Senate, the U.S. annually provides Ukraine with $225 million dollars that are conditioned on "Ukrainian implementation of radical economic reforms which are the continuation of the previous reforms." This constitutes the third largest package of U.S. foreign aid after Israel (3 billion dollars annually) and Egypt (2 billion dollars annually).

The process of giving aid to Ukraine has been anything but smooth. In fall-winter 1995 the U.S. administration and international financial organizations expressed their concern about the decreasing speed of reforms, and of privatization in particular, in Ukraine. There was a threat of a sharp reduction or even cancellation of certain aid programs, which coincided with the postponement in spring 1996 of the realization of a 1.5 billion dollars standby IMF credit. Thanks only to the efforts of Ukrainian President Kuchma during his working visit to Washington in February 1996 that his American partners and leaders of international financial organizations were persuaded that Ukrainian political and economic reforms would not be reversed. In May 1996 Ukraine resumed receiving the next installments of the standby credit worth of 900 million dollars. In sum, during 1994–1996 Ukraine received more than 1.5 billion dollars from the IMF.

Now we can look forward to receiving up to 3 billion dollars of Extended Fund Facility (EFF) credit. The World Bank is a valuable Ukrainian partner in Washington because it gives preferential (17-years term, minimal annual rate) credits for important restructural programs in coal industry, energy, inter-city management and agriculture. In June 1996 the Board of Directors of the World Bank decided to give Ukraine a first 310 million-dollar loan for its structural reforms. All in all the World Bank has given Ukraine more than 600 million dollars worth of credits.

American governmental aid reaches Ukraine through the United States Agency for International Development (USAID) that has its office in Kyiv (headed by Gregory Huger) and provides a number of programs in such areas as the development of energy sector, structural reformation of the financial-banking system, development of the private sector, democratic reforms, development of social security sector, privatization programs, reforms in the housing and municipal management, medical and environmental aid and others.

Owing to USAID programs thousands of Ukrainian specialists could visit the United States and acquaint themselves with the American experience in various spheres of political and economic life. Ukrainian officials have often declared their gratitude for the programs and for the generous aid, but in 1995–1996 they also expressed some ideas for ways of streamlining the USAID programs with regard to the three priorities formulated by President Kuchma and Prime Minister Lazarenko during their visits to the United States: structural reforms and modernization of the energy sector (a program tentatively named "Energy independence of Ukraine"); development of an agricultural-industrial sector; development of small business and entrepreneurship.

One of the vitally important spheres of cooperation between Ukraine and the United States is attracting American investments in the Ukrainian economy. Although the amount of foreign investments in Ukraine for the beginning of 1996 will reach one billion dollars (American companies' share is 250 million dollars), this sum is minuscule as compared to the foreign investments in the Russian (4 billion dollars), Polish (4 billion dollars), or Hungarian (5 billion dollars) economies.

A very important factor in encouraging U.S. investment in Ukrainian economy is the Overseas Private Investment Corporation (OPIC), an independent federal agency that finances investments, covers them against political risks and provides services to the investors. OPIC operates in almost 140 countries, among them Ukraine, providing our country with financial help and insurance policies worth over 40 million dollars, which, in fact, is not much compared to the general amount of its U.S. domestic financial (1.8 billion dollars) and insurance (8.6 billion dollars) operations in the 1995 fiscal year. Among the main preconditions for attracting American investors, our American partners name the creation of a favorable climate for investment in Ukraine which includes reforming the tax system, political and social stability in the country, curbing bribery and red tape, and a professional approach to presenting investment opportunities in order to convince potential investors of the profitability of certain projects and sites. In fact it is only in 1996 that Ukrainians who wish to attract foreign capital finally moved from general declarations to concrete projects. A number of investment conferences were held in Houston, Los Angeles, Washington, DC, Kyiv, and Crimea. At these conferences Ukrainian participants presented over 300 investment projects in the fields of energy industry, machine-building, housing and municipal management, hotel business and defense conversion. Hundreds of American companies—from giants like General Motors, Motorola, and Cargill, to small private businesses that view Ukraine as a potential investment bonanza, took part in these conferences. The adoption of the Ukrainian Constitution, especially those articles that guarantee the right of private ownership, including land ownership, was welcomed by U.S. business circles and this hopefully will invigorate investment in the Ukrainian economy.

Trade between Ukraine and the United States (not including services) in 1995 reached the level of 632 million dollars, which is 24% more than in 1994. Throughout 1995 it was constantly on the rise, albeit at the expense of increasing of import into Ukraine. In 1995 Ukrainian exports to the United States were 82 million dollars (25%) more than the previous year and exceeded Ukrainian imports from the United States (the difference being 186 million dollars).

The most perceptible areas of Ukrainian exports to the United States were ferrous metals (229.4 million dollars or 56.15% in Ukrainian export to the United States) and clothes (62.6 million dollars—15.3%). Ukraine imported mainly machines, equipment, mechanical devices (67.6 million dollars—30.3% in overall import), land transport means (20.4 million dollars—9.2%), and electrical equipment (15.0 million dollars—6.6%). Among goods that were imported in smaller quantities were grain, meat, beverages, paper, and furniture.

U.S.-Ukrainian military-political cooperation has been especially procutive, both bilaterally and within the framework of the NATO "Partnership for Peace" (PfP) program which Ukraine, the first of the CIS countries, joined in February 8, 1994.

Within the framework of this program Ukrainian military units participated in four multinational PfP exercises on the territory of Ukraine and United States. Also, in accordance with the bilateral agreement joint U.S.-Ukrainian marine exercises were conducted during 1995–1996 in Ukraine and in the United States. During these exercises joint peace-keeping operations were carried out and both sides gained considerable experience in combat cooperation. For 1996, the U.S. allotted 10 million dollars to support Ukrainian participation in the PfP program. That enabled the Ukrainian Armed Forces to become fully engaged in the first stage of the PfP program with a minimal burden to the national budget.

The bilateral cooperation between the Ukrainian and American departments of defense is the United States' most active relationship with an East-Central European country. In 1995 the majority of CIS and East-Central European students in U.S. military academies were Ukrainian officers. It would be no exaggeration to state that for the past several years relations between the leaders of the Ukrainian Defense Ministry and the American Defense Department have been friendly, business-like, and trusting. Special credit here must go to U.S. Secretary of Defense William Perry, who greatly contributed to the strengthening of this cooperation. Mr. Perry proudly displays in his Pentagon office photographs of his numerous trips to Ukraine. Annual elaborate plans of cooperation between the defense departments of our countries are being worked out and implemented with military precision. And this successful experience laid the foundation for the idea of future deepening cooperation between various corresponding ministries and agencies.

Space cooperation between Ukraine and the United States is based on agreements on cooperation in peaceful space exploration and on joint declarations on future commercial cooperation in aerospace (1994, 1996). This resulted in the use of Ukrainian rocket carriers in the international consortium "Sea Launch" project, whose co-founders are the Ukrainian "Southern" (Pivdenne) Design Bureau, PMZ Machine-building Factory (Dnipropetrovsk, Ukraine), the American Boeing Corporation, the Norwegian corporation "Kwerner," and the Russian company "Energija."

NASA cooperates with Ukraine in the fields of space biology and microgravitation, telecommunication, telemedicine, and space welding. In 1997 a Ukrainian cosmonaut will fly in one of the space-shuttle missions and conduct scientific experiments.

Despite our desire for them to be more extensive, our cooperation in medicine, pharmacology, in solving Chernobyl-connected problems, in environmental studies, and in cultural and educational exchanges is less active than in other areas. Inter-regional cooperation is slow to start, although there are exceptions here: twin-city relations between Kyiv and Chicago celebrated its five-year anniversary with "Kyiv days in Chicago." Steady relations are growing between Cherkassy Oblast and Iowa. Among the promising projects in this area is setting up contacts between Crimea and Florida.

The Role of the Ukrainian Embassy in Strengthening Relations with the United States

In a picturesque section of Washington, on the banks of the Potomac River, not far from Georgetown University there is a building complex that belongs to Ukraine. It is here, at the crossroads of M Street and 34th that the Ukrainian Embassy is located. One of the Embassy buildings is a historical sight—it is in this house that the first American President George Washington stayed in 1791. The great Ukrainian poet Taras Shevchenko wrote over a hundred years ago, in 1857, the prophetic words:

> You miserable crew, when will you breath your last?
> When shall we get ourselves a Washington
> With a new and just law?
> But some day we shall surely find him.

That is why, as a token of our respect to one of the greatest sons of the United States, we have decided to open a memorial Washington room and to decorate it with historic items as well as portraits of George Washington and Taras Shevchenko. And this historic parallel seems particularly relevant on the eve of the fifth anniversary of establishing diplomatic relations between Ukraine and the United States.

The Ukrainian embassy in the United States is an important governmental unit staffed by employees of the Ministry of Foreign Affairs, Ministry of Foreign Economic and Trade Relations, Ministry of Defense, and others. The embassy is carrying out its everyday, multifaceted, often tedious but highly necessary job of defending the political and economic interests of Ukraine and Ukrainian citizens, of securing the implementation of the foreign policy guidelines of the president of Ukraine, and the orders and instructions of the Ministry of Foreign Affairs as the sole coordinating foreign policy organ of Ukraine. In the United States now there is a network of Ukrainian diplomatic offices which includes the Ukrainian embassy, the Ukrainian UN representation, consulars general in New York and Chicago and an affiliated office of the Ukrainian trade mission in Los Angeles. Beginning in 1994, which marked a turning point in Ukrainian-American relations, the embassy in Washington increased the amount and volume of its informational and analytical input. It performs the daily monitoring of domestic life and foreign activities of the United States. Special attention is paid to the 1996 American presidential campaign. We have strengthened contacts with the State Department, the National Security Council, the Congress, the Ukrainian-American community, political and analytical centers, funds and universities where the ideologies and analyses underlying U.S. foreign policy are being formulated. We have widely used roundtable discussions of the current issues of Ukrainian internal and foreign policy with the participation of Ukrainian government officials and members of Parliament. We also invite American officials, congressmen, influential analysts and journalists. During the period of 1995–1996 we have had over 50 roundtable discussions on the constitutional process in Ukraine, the character and speed of economic reforms, issues of European security and NATO expansion as well as problems related to the Chornobyl catastrophe.

Five Years Behind Us…What is in Store?

The next anniversary—ten years of established diplomatic relations between Ukraine and the United States—will be celebrated in 2002. What will the world of the beginning of the twenty-first century be like? Without risking being called a false prophet, one can safely claim that the amount of international problems as well as armed conflicts will only increase. The front lines of tomorrow are easily perceived now and, unfortunately, they have the tendency to explode every now and then.

At the dawn of Ukrainian independence, in a book published in 1918, the first President of Ukraine Mykhailo S. Hrushevskyi, contemplating the directions of the foreign policy of the Ukrainian National Republic, wrote these prophetic words:

> For our future America undoubtedly has great importance—because of its enormous financial and technical means, but also as a school for the future generations of our technicians, economists, and social workers. The cadre of our workers and politicians can learn a lot from this people because Americans are more democratic than any other European nation, more industrious, and more outgoing in the realization of their dreams and plans. The Ukrainians who went out to colonize America are numerous and at this moment particularly enthusiastic about helping our revival. They can truly be of great help for the New Ukraine.

Eighty years later Hrushevskyi's dreams have come true. The official Ukrainian-American communiqué, signed on September 19, 1996, that announces the setting up of the Commission of Ukrainian-American Cooperation, headed by President Kuchma and Vice-President Gore, for the first time uses the term "strategic partnership" between our countries.

The fall 1996 visits to Washington of the Secretary of the Council of National Security and Defense Volodymyr Horbulin and Ukrainian Foreign Minister Hennadiy Udovenko helped to fill this wide formula with concrete meaning. The strategic partnership envisages a closer co-operation in various fields, including national security, foreign policy, economy, trade, investments and in other directions where Ukrainian and the U.S. interests coincide.

What will Ukrainian-American relations be like in the years 2002, 2010, 2020? Will they reach the level of a full-fledged partnership similar to those that exist between the United States and Israel, or, like a pendulum, contrary to the common sense and the logic of history, will they move in the opposite direction? We have to think about it today, while preparing a long-term concept of Ukrainian-American relations in accordance with the strategic goal of our foreign policy formulated by President Kuchma: in the twenty-first century Ukraine must integrate into the European Community and become a full and legitimate member of the Trans-Atlantic community of countries and nations.

We often quote a banal English aphorism: a country has no permanent friends, it has permanent interests. I believe that it is in the permanent interest of Ukraine to have trustworthy and steady allies and friends. And the United States of America should be one of these well-deserved, permanent allies.

Six

The National and Legal Status of the Ukrainian City of Sevastopol and Problems of the Black Sea Division*

Thank you for the opportunity to present the official position of the Ukrainian Government in connection with the serious aggravation of the situation around Sevastopol.

The question centers on the latest decisions of the highest Russian legislative bodies with regard to the status of Sevastopol and the fate of the Black Sea Fleet. I would like to remind you that this case is not a new one. In July, 1993, the Duma of the Russian Federation adopted a resolution "On the Status of the City of Sevastopol," which stated that Sevastopol had federal status within Russia. That resolution, which aggressively violated universally recognized principles and norms of international law, in particular Paragraph 4 of Article 2 of the United Nations Charter, as well as resolutions of the OSCE and provisions of the Treaty between Ukraine and Russia of November 19, 1990, was condemned by the world community, including the United States of America and by the UN Security Council, which distributed a special statement on this matter on July 20, 1993:

> The Security Council reaffirms in this connection its commitment to the territorial integrity of Ukraine, in accordance with the Charter of the United Nations. The Security Council recalls that in the Treaty between the Russian Federation and Ukraine, signed at Kiev on 19 November 1990, the High Contracting Parties committed themselves to respect each other's territorial integrity within their currently existing frontiers. The Decree of the Supreme Soviet of the Russian Federation is incompatible with this commitment as well as with the

* Delivered at the Center for Strategic and International Studies (Washington, DC, December 10, 1996)

purposes and principles of the Charter of the United Nations, and without effect.

On July 10, 1993 the U.S. ambassador to Ukraine stated on this issue, "The United States notes President Kravchuk's statement on the Russian Parliament's action concerning good bilateral relations with Russia. This is no time for the Russian Parliament to be attempting to strain that relationship. The United States supports the territorial integrity of all boundaries under the Helsinki Accords. Sevastopol is an integral part of Ukraine."

It seemed at that time that the most serious episode of "Sevastopol fever" had passed. Then a long and not so simple, yet peaceful process of negotiations proceeded. The process of Ukrainian-Russian negotiations on the Black Sea Fleet problem began in 1992 with the Yalta Agreement. A significant breakthrough was achieved in Sochi on July 9, 1995. Main principles for the Black Sea Fleet were determined and in the end of this year and during the first half of 1996 actual division started.

To our regret, for many reasons in the fall of 1996 the second stage of the so-called "Sevastopol campaign" began. The initiators of this campaign were influential political leaders and parties of Russia, such as General Aleksandr Lebed—then Chief of the Russian Security Council—and Moscow Mayor Yurii Luzhkov, as well as others. The Ukrainian leadership, in turn, demonstrated patience and deliberation and tried to avoid confrontation even after the Russian Duma adopted the law "On Cessation of the Black Sea Fleet Division" in its first reading on October 16, 1996.

According to information of the Russian mass-media, the arguments of certain Russian politicians are as follows:

- Political abandonment of the campaign by Russia to claim Sevastopol as Russian territory would negatively impact on the internal position of the Russian government, would demonstrate its inability to defend its national interests, and therefore to tackle the task of contemporary Russian nation-building.
- If Russia should renounce Sevastopol as a Russian city, a precedent of resolving territorial disputes in a manner inconsistent with legal procedures would be created. It would lead to the development of centrifugal tendencies in Russia which may cause dissolution of the nation.

- In its international aspect, securing the southern border of Russia and the CIS, the level of Russia's influence on the Black Sea region, as well as on the international arena as a whole, depend in great measure on the settlement of the problems of Sevastopol and the Black Sea Fleet.
- Keeping Sevastopol within Russia would significantly improve its geopolitical situation and would provide for the stabilization of the internal situation in Russia.
- From the point of view of national and cultural traditions in Russia, Sevastopol is one of the strategic elements of Russian national consciousness. The loss of Sevastopol would not only damage patriotic feelings of the Russian people but would complicate the process of searching for a new national identity which is very important now in connection with the rebirth of Russian statehood.

It is not difficult to see that these arguments are based not on principles of international law but represent purely political tools. Until now we have proceeded from the assumption that the Duma, which is known for its opposition to the Russian Executive, does not reflect the official position of Russia. We view as legitimate the positions only of President Yeltsin, Prime Minister Chernomyrdin and Russian Foreign Minister Primakov, who have clearly and repeatedly stated that the Ukrainian status of Sevastopol is indisputable and that the process of division should be accomplished with previous bilateral agreements.

However, on December 5, 1996, the Federation Council, the upper chamber of the Russian Parliament, approved decisions that can only be viewed as territorial claims on Ukraine and a violation of all previous agreements on the Black Sea Fleet division. The Federation Council adopted a legislative package, in particular "The Statement on the Status of Sevastopol" aimed at proclaiming Russian status of the Ukrainian city of Sevastopol. In essence, the Russian Federation has raised territorial claims on Ukraine and infringes upon its sovereignty.

The Federation Council also approved an appeal to the presidents of Russia and Ukraine to preserve the unity of the Black Sea Fleet. The gravity of the situation and potential danger of these decisions lies in the fact that some representatives of the Russian executive branch are also members of the Federation Council—governors of Russian provinces—who, by and large, were nominated by the Russian president and who cannot be accused of acting in opposition to President Yeltsin.

In reply to these decisions by the Federation Council the Parliament of Ukraine on December 6 of this year approved a resolution which states that it considers such actions by the Duma as:

> ...a gross violation of fundamental norms of international law, encroachment on the sovereignty of Ukraine:
>
> By its recent actions the Russian side has aggravated the situation to the utmost. In view of such unfriendly actions of the Russian Federation's Federal Assembly, the Verkhovna Rada [Parliament] of Ukraine makes a resolute protest against falsifications, specifically around the status of the city of Sevastopol, which is an inalienable part of Ukraine, rejects any territorial claims on Ukraine and views them as a deliberate undermining of European security.
>
> The Verkhovna Rada of Ukraine declares that Sevastopol has been and shall remain Ukrainian territory. No one in Ukraine shall ever carry on any negotiations which would contradict the Constitution of Ukraine, its legislation, its national interests, and which would lead to its territorial disintegration.
>
> Proceeding from the aforesaid, the Verkhovna Rada of Ukraine introduces the draft Bill on withdrawal of Russian troops from the territory of Ukraine and appeals to international institutions on grounds of infringement upon our sovereignty.

Let me give a brief account of the main points of our position:

1. According to Article 17 of the Constitution of Ukraine "Foreign military bases may not be located on the territory of Ukraine." Taking into consideration the real situation in Sevastopol on the day of adoption of the Constitution—June 28, 1996—Paragraph 14 of the Transitional Provisions was adopted stipulating that "the use of existing military bases on the territory of Ukraine for the temporary deployment of foreign military formations is permissible on the basis of leasing terms described in international treaties of Ukraine, ratified by the Verkhovna Rada of Ukraine."

2. All the historical materials on the national and legal status of Sevastopol which we have distributed here testify to the indisputable status of Sevastopol as a Ukrainian city. With regard to the USSR's law "On the transfer of the Crimean Oblast from the Russian Federation to the Ukrainian S.S.R." of April 26, 1954, I would like to underline that the Crimean Oblast as a whole was transferred to Ukraine. This included the city of Sevastopol.

Since 1954, Sevastopol has been an integral part of Ukraine in all areas of the state and political life, be it in its subordination, in the day-to-day activities of its executive and representative bodies, in the funding from the Ukrainian state budget, etc. The current status was codified in the Soviet constitutions of the Russian Federation and Ukraine in 1978 which placed Moscow and Leningrad in the list of cities of republican subordination in Russia, while Kyiv and Sevastopol were considered cities of republican subordination in Ukraine.

Let me also offer some personal observations. When I was minister of environmental protection of Ukraine, prior to the dissolution of the USSR, I paid a lot of attention specifically to ecological problems of Sevastopol as a Ukrainian city. The environmental authorities in Sevastopol were subordinated to me and we instituted control over the ecological activity of the Black Sea Fleet, which had caused a great deal of damage to the Black Sea basin. The lack of drinking water has been and remains one of the most dramatic problems in Sevastopol since its natural water reservoirs have been exhausted. This problem can be solved only through delivery of water from the Dnieper River to the Crimea.

Neither before, nor during the dissolution of the USSR did anyone, I emphasize, anyone either in Sevastopol, or in Moscow, ever raise the question of the Russian status of the city. This issue was invented by those who desire to complicate the situation in the region, as well as in Europe as a whole.

3. As it is well known, 80–90% of the Black Sea Fleet of the former USSR was deployed in Sevastopol. The Soviet Union viewed this naval base as an important bridge-head for the hypothetical seizure of the Black Sea straits in conjunction with a ground offensive of Soviet troops. The Black Sea Fleet was designed to provide strategic offensive actions not only on the Black Sea but also in the Mediterranean theater of war.

With the collapse of the Soviet empire this function of Sevastopol has ceased to exist. Ukraine has no plans for military confrontation with its Black Sea neighbors. Moreover, it does not envisage any future military operations in the Mediterranean.

The Ukrainian Navy operates on the basis of a defensive military doctrine. Its main task is to defend the southern sea borders of Ukraine in the area of the Black Sea.

I would like to remind you that there is no historical precedent in which a single fleet ever served two states, especially two states with divergent interests. I would also like to mention that the Caspian fleet of the former Soviet Navy was divided among Russia, Azerbaijan, and Kazakhstan.

All these facts prove that the idea to suspend the division of the Black Sea Fleet and establish a joint Russian-Ukrainian fleet does not make sense and has no legal, political, or military grounds. As Ukrainian Minister of Defense Oleksander Kuzmuk stated on December 6, 1996, "there cannot be any joint command."

4. According to the Sochi arrangements between the presidents of Ukraine and Russia of June 9, 1995, vessels and other moveable property should be divided equally. At the same time Ukraine will retain 18.3% of the Black Sea Fleet battleships and 31.7% of battleships will be transferred to Russia on the basis of compensation. And we shall abide by these principles in the future.

Let me emphasize that before Russia ceased implementation of the arrangements concerning the fleet's division, this process was proceeding rather successfully.

As of now, the Ukrainian Navy has more than 70 ships and vessels which, are deployed in Sevastopol, Odesa, Kerch, and Ochakiv. As soon as the division of the fleet is accomplished, the quantity of ships and vessels in the Ukrainian Navy will reach about 150 units. According to the Sochi agreement from June 9, 1995, the main base of the Russian Black Sea Fleet will be located in the city of Sevastopol and basing of the two fleets shall be separate. The Russian side, arbitrarily interpreting the above provision, insists that:

1. The entire city of Sevastopol be the base of the Russian Black Sea Fleet. This is a demonstration of territorial and property claims on the Ukrainian city of Sevastopol and on its ground infrastructure which belong to Ukraine.

2. The Russian side objects to the deployment of the Ukrainian Navy Headquarters and the main base of the Ukrainian Navy in Sevastopol.

In connection with this I would note that the sea-based facilities of Sevastopol are such that allow the Ukrainian and Russian fleets to operate independently of each other. This is adequately illustrated by reviewing any map of Sevastopol. Besides this we have examples from international practice, for example, the military and naval base in Subic-Bay, (Philippines) where Philippine and American fleets are based together. Another example is Naples which serves as a base jointly for the American and Italian navies.

No person and no state has a right to dictate to Ukraine where it should deploy its navy on its own territory. The question of deployment of the Ukrainian Navy's headquarters and battleships is not a subject of negotiations. This is purely an internal matter of Ukraine.

The decisions by Russia's Federation Council was very seriously taken by the leadership of Ukraine and by Ukrainian public opinion. The Ukrainian leadership has approached the developing situation with extreme care.

President Leonid Kuchma of Ukraine is in full control of the situation, while the National Security and Defense Council has prepared a packet of documents which outline the necessary countermeasures.

We appeal to the world community—to the UN, OSCE, Council of Europe, Black Sea Cooperation Council, leaders of friendly countries, including the U.S., to take all measures in order to convince Russia that the path of territorial claims is counterproductive.

We would certainly not wish that certain Russian politicians, for the sake of their ambitious aspirations and neo-imperial illusions, would cause irreperable damage to friendly relations between the Ukrainian and Russian people.

The Ukrainian leadership will do its best not to allow the situation to be aggravated as far as it could be. We will not allow this situation to be used as a reason for disagreements and hostilities between our states and peoples. We are ready to continue negotiating the basic Ukrainian-Russian treaty on friendship and cooperation. We also wish to jointly solve the problems of economic cooperation between our countries.

We believe that political wisdom and common sense will in the long run prevail.

Seven

Ukrainian Foreign Policy toward Israel*

I will try to give you a couple of thoughts and facts on the topic of Ukrainian-Israeli relations, according to my own experience as a former ambassador of Ukraine to the State of Israel.

I left this vitally important country in October 1994. Since 1994, Israel has experienced a number of great changes: changes in the peace process in the Middle East, changes of state leadership, and so on. Considering the whole complex of Ukrainian-Jewish relations we should delineate two separate issues: First, the relationship between the Ukrainian and Jewish peoples, which has existed for over a millennium and abounds in many different events, including several periods of bloody conflicts. Second, the relationship between our two countries, which is very brief, given the fact that it begins only in 1991 with the recognition of our country by Israel.

We highly appreciate the fact that the State of Israel was one of the first to establish diplomatic relations with Ukraine—on the 26th of December 1991—25 days after the all-Ukrainian referendum in which 92% of the voters supported the independence of Ukraine. However, the first diplomatic contacts between Ukrainian and Israeli representatives took place earlier—at the UN and through unofficial channels. In October 1992 the Embassy of Ukraine was opened in Israel. I was the first ambassador. Later, in January 1993, the Embassy of Israel was established in Kyiv. In September 1993 the first Israeli ambassador to Ukraine, Mr. Zvi Magen, was nominated.

The visit of President Leonid Kravchuk to Israel in January 11–13, 1993 became the first summit of our leaders. It was the beginning of a new stage in Ukrainian-Jewish relations directed toward the future. These relations have been founded on the principles of equality, mutual

---

*   Remarks at the Conference "Ukraine in the World" (George Washington University, December 12, 1996)

understanding, respect, benefit, and non-interference in the internal affairs of each other. Six intergovernmental agreements that were signed in 1993 have become a good basis for our common future relations. The main ones—especially the "Memorandum on the Principles of Relations between Ukraine and Israel," signed January 12, 1993—envisages regular consultations on issues of foreign policy.

The legal basis for relations in agriculture, science, technology, culture and international air transportation was laid down in those agreements. Let me stress that the attitude of Israeli authorities toward relationships with all friendly states—not only with Ukraine—is specific, and it can be expressed by the words said of the former foreign minister of Israel Mr. Shimon Peres. In 1994 he pointed out that for Israel Ukraine is the most important state out of the three or four countries with the largest Jewish communities. Mr. Peres said:

> The Jewish community in Ukraine is a very significant investment of Israel in Ukraine, because the State of Israel is not only the state for its citizens, but also it is a state for all Jewish people. We want the relations between Israel and Ukraine to become as similar as the relations between Israel and the U.S.... I mean, we have good relations with both—the U.S. government and the U.S.-Jewish community... Ukraine is not only a state for us, but also is our memory...

Mr. Peres declared that the present situation of Jews in Ukraine as reported by the newspapers differed from the truth as much as the east differs from the west. When delivering a lecture at the Kyiv Institute for Foreign Relations, Mr. Peres said that the "hunting season" in rhetoric on Ukrainian-Jewish relations had ended and nothing could be reached by such a war of words. A new future is being born on the ruins of the Cold War, Mr. Peres invoked, so that, "we must not stand on the balconies of the past, but we must stand on the threshold of the future."

Let me briefly inform you of some data about the Ukrainian-Jewish community given to me by the Council of Jewish Organizations of Ukraine. The official figure is more than 500,000. Most of them—95%—live in big cities—Kyiv, Dnipropetrovsk, Odesa, and Kharkiv. Unfortunately, the Jewish population in small towns (*mistechkos*), especially in Galicia, has practically disappeared. Only 10% of Jews in Ukraine know Yiddish, almost nobody knows Hebrew, 40% know Ukrainian and 90% know Russian. In Ukraine two large associations for

Jews now exist which unite more than 100 Jewish communities. There are more than 50 synagogues and 70 Jewish schools including 3 state schools. More than 20 religious Jewish societies have been established. Special programs rendering aid to potential repatriates and old and sick people are being carried out by the "Sohnut" and "Joint" organizations, which operate completely legally in Ukraine. The International Solomon University opened in Kyiv and is attended by 300 students, 100 of which are Jews.

The policy of the government of Ukraine aims at strengthening the friendship and building confidence between the Ukrainian and Jewish peoples. We are building truly friendly relations and a special partnership with Israel. This was convincingly proved during the latest official visit of Ukrainian President Leonid Kuchma to Israel in November, 1996, which became an important milestone in our relations. President Kuchma, speaking at the forum of the Israeli Knesset, confirmed that in its Middle-East policy Ukraine resolutely rejects the ideological dogmas of the former Soviet relationship with the countries of the region. Ukraine instead supports the search for a mutual compromise among all parties involved in the Middle East conflict, with full implementation of respective UN resolutions. "We call upon all parties," stressed President Kuchma, "to refrain from violence, to continue the process of peaceful settlement on the basis of mutually accepted compromises. Ukraine is ready to take appropriate part in the activity of multilateral working groups on arms control and national security, on economic cooperation, on water resources, ecological issues, and on the issue of Palestinian refugees."

Using its political prestige and its geopolitical situation in the world Ukraine has tried to play an intermediary role in Middle-East settlement in Arab-Israeli relations. During his visit to Israel, President Kuchma conducted productive negotiations with Israeli President Ezer Weizman, Prime Minister Binyamin Netanyahu, Foreign Minister David Levy. At the negotiations Israeli leaders underscored the fact that Ukraine and Israel have common historical roots. The 300,000 Ukrainian Jews who have emigrated to Israel have contributed significantly to the development of the country.

President Kuchma stressed that Ukraine can usefully cooperate in the field of new technologies, air-space industry, ship-building, chemical industry, etc. President Kuchma also met with Chairman Yasser Arafat in Bethlehem and they agreed upon establishing a PLO political representation in Ukraine.

The president of Ukraine has initiated an important concept with the creation of a strategic tripartite relationship of Ukraine, the United States, and Israel. We hope that this special partnership, which is now being discussed among our countries, can become an important instrument in world policy. The idea of establishing such a tripartite relationship still requires deep study and respective elaboration. In my opinion, cooperation among our three countries can develop productively, in particular, in such fields as the Middle-East settlement; economic, financial, and trade cooperation; military-technical cooperation; the struggle against international terrorism, organized crime, illegal traffic, and money laundering; agriculture; and humanitarian cooperation.

As a former ambassador to Israel and current ambassador to the United States, I am ready to contribute personally to the development of this kind of relationship.

EIGHT

A Meeting with the House Legislative Assistants Association*

The Ukrainian Government, our embassy, and I are personally paying significant attention to the development of good relations with the U.S. Congress, its members, and staff. We understand the importance and influence of this institution as the highest legislative power in one of the world's oldest democracies. I have many friends in the U.S. Congress and am very proud of that fact.

The U.S. Congress is playing a very important role in the positive development of the Ukrainian-American relations. You know better than I do that the year 1996 in the activity of the U.S. Congress was full of many important events related to elections and internal matters. Nevertheless, the U.S. Congress paid significant attention to the development of Ukrainian-American relations.

I would like to list some of the actions taken by the U.S. Congress with regard to Ukraine:

1. In February, 1996, President Leonid Kuchma, during his official visit to Washington, had a meeting with the Senate Foreign Relations Committee, chaired by Senator Jesse Helms (R-NC).

2. In April, the Commission on Security and Cooperation in Europe held hearings commemorating the 10th Anniversary of the Chornobyl Catastrophe.

3. In May, the House of Representatives endorsed Resolution H.Con.Res. 167 commemorating the 10th Anniversary of Chornobyl.

4. In July, Prime Minister Lazarenko had a meeting with the House International Committee chaired by Congressman Benjamin Gilman (R-NY).

---

* Remarks at the Embassy of Ukraine (Washington, DC, February 5, 1997).

5. On September 4, the House approved Resolution H.Con. Res. 120, supporting the sovereignty and independence of Ukraine.

6. On September 30, President Clinton enacted the Foreign Operations Appropriation Act which earmarked $225 million as the U.S. assistance to Ukraine under the Freedom Support Act. This earmark put Ukraine in third place among recipient countries of U.S. foreign aid, after Israel and Egypt.

I believe that this gathering here is very special for you as legislative staff because this building has a historical connection with the beginning of legislative process in your country. It was in this building that George Washington endorsed the decision to establish the District of Columbia. And now our embassy is working to recreate the George Washington historical room, where we also intend to display copies of some historical documents and laws related to this event.

Tonight let me say a few words about Ukraine, the country and its government, which I have the honor to represent here in the United States of America. I would like to inform you of the internal political and economic situation in my country and of the present status of Ukrainian-American relations.

Last year we celebrated a very remarkable event for my country: the fifth anniversary of Ukraine's independence. Despite all the past and present difficulties in our development, Ukraine has, in the past five years, made significant strides towards building a stable democracy and successful economy. These achievements become more visible when contrasted with developments in other countries which emerged after the collapse of the Soviet Union.

Since it became an independent nation five years ago, Ukraine has:

1. Become free of inter-ethnic and inter-regional conflicts.

2. Become the first country of the region to provide a peaceful transition of executive power: from the presidency of Leonid Kravchuk to that of incumbent President Leonid Kuchma.

3. Removed all nuclear armaments from its territory, governed by its own good will, and thus made a major contribution to global peace and security.

4. Been accepted as a member of the Council of Europe and the NATO Partnership for Peace program.

5. Introduced major economic reforms despite the extreme hardship for its citizens.

6. Adopted a new constitution which corresponds to the international standards for democratic states and meets the requirements of the Council of Europe.

7. Become a strategically important state between East and West, and become recognized by the U.S. and the European Community.

8. Established relations of strategic partnership last year with the United States.

9. Become, as I have already mentioned, the number three nation after Israel and Egypt in the amount of allocated U.S. foreign aid.

During its five years of independence, the most significant event for our country has been the adoption of the new Ukrainian Constitution on June 28, 1996. Thus the legal basis for the further realization of economic reforms in our country, including the improvement of its foreign trade regime and investment climate, was constructed. The Constitution made a substantial departure from the Soviet political system and communist ideology and strove in its stead to create a free market economy and to establish a state governed by the rule of law. One of the most prominent features of this document is that it guarantees the right to won private property, including land. Now we have the task of adopting nearly two hundred new laws, rules and regulations, including commercial law and a civil code.

The adoption of Ukraine's Constitution proved the following:

1. Ukraine and its people reached a political consensus regarding the further movement towards democracy.

2. The Constitution reconfirmed the will of the Ukrainian people to build an independent state guided by Western values of freedom, democracy, law and order.

3. Ukraine has a democratic political elite capable of running the nation in a democratic manner.

4. The adoption of the Ukrainian Constitution was a heavy blow to communists and other radical leftists in Ukraine and abroad who dreamed about the restoration of the Soviet Empire and of communist ideology.

5. It was a dramatic act of national reconciliation and consolidation and provided an additional element of stability for our state and society.

According to its constitution, Ukraine is a sovereign and independent, democratic, social and legal state in which rule of law exists and is recognized. Ukraine is a unitarian state and has single citizenship.

The administrative and territorial structure of Ukraine includes the Autonomous Republic of Crimea which has a right to its own constitution, which must be adopted by the Crimean Parliament and approved by the Verhkhovna Rada (Parliament) of Ukraine by no less than one-half of the members of the national parliament.

The Constitution provides for a mixed presidental-parliamentary form of government.

The highest legislative power is vested in the Parliament of Ukraine, known in Ukrainian as the Verkhovna Rada. The Parliament is made up of 450 deputies who are elected for a term of four years.

The president of Ukraine is the head of state and speaks on its behalf. The president is also the guarantor of the state sovereignty and the territorial integrity of the state.

The Constitution provides for political, economic, and ideological diversity. No ideology can be considered mandatory by the State. It prohibits censorship and guarantees freedom of political activity. It also ensures an independent foreign policy of Ukraine based on the generally acknowledged principles of international law.

I should emphasize that very positive developments have been made in Ukraine in the area of human rights. According to a special report of the State Department, Ukraine has had a very good record with regard to human rights for the last five years. We also are witnessing the rapid development of the Ukrainian political and party systems. During the last five years, hundreds of political parties and movements have emerged both on the all-national and local levels. At the national level alone, our Ministry of Justice has registered more than 40 political parties and movements with a very broad spectrum of political doctrines and views, ranging from the radical right, which is represented by ultranationalists, to the radical left, which is represented by communist forces that stand for communist ideology and the re-creation of the former USSR. We also have witnessed the creation of "exotic" political parties, such as the Party of Beer Lovers.

So now we could say that the Ukrainian people are not as single-minded as they were considered five years ago. Democratic political reforms in Ukraine stimulated quick development of public and professional organizations. The single National Trade Union, which was previously controlled by the Soviet Communist Party Politburo, spontaneously disintegrated as soon as the party collapsed. Now we have 29 independent trade unions which represent the interests of every professional community or respective region.

After having been suppressed by the KGB for many years, religious organizations in Ukraine have recently witnessed a true boom in their growth. Ukraine has become the home of dozens of religions and denominations. They include Orthodox, Catholic, Presbyterian, Methodist, Jewish, Islamic, Mormon, and many other faiths and denominations. Compared to the Soviet period, the number of denominations registered in Ukraine has grown from 18 to over 60, and the number of religious communities has grown three times and now numbers 15,000. We are likewise proud to state that there are no ethnic conflicts in our country, which is a very spectacular achievement given that we have nearly 130 ethnic groups. Unfettered conditions have been created for the heritage-based and religious activities of ethnic minorities.

As you may know, Ukraine has introduced a number of drastic economic measures, many of which were politically very difficult. We have turned the macroeconomic situation in the country around. The privatization of small and medium size enterprises is practically complete. Our private sector is made up of some 36,000 companies which produce over 50% of the GDP. With respect to our large enterprises, the government has slated for privatization over 200 enterprises in such key sectors of our economy as energy, metallurgy, and machine-building. Foreign capital is welcome in every sector of our economy.

One of our major economic achievements in 1996 was the emergence of a viable banking sector. Today over 200 commercial banks operate in Ukraine, including six large banks and seventeen banks with foreign capital. There are also examples in Ukraine of successful activity conducted by foreign banks such as Credit Lyonnais and Deutschebank. Recently the Government of Ukraine made a decision to issue the first release of Euro bonds.

We also are witnessing a rapid development of Ukraine's stock market. Today there are almost 15 million share-holders in Ukraine. Considerable success was achieved in the activity of the Ukrainian Central Stock Exchange, which is constantly increasing the volume of its operations. At the same time, other stock exchanges are also vigorously developing. The successful creation of the national stock market has been promoted by the Government of Ukraine, which ensured free transfer of interests and profits in hard currency from the territory of Ukraine.

Another considerable achievement was the macrostabilization of the Ukrainian finance system. We have brought inflation under control from 10,000% a year in 1993, to 39.7% in 1996.[1] This has allowed us to introduce the new national currency, the "hryvnia," last September and to preserve its stability. This result would have been impossible without the support we have received form the IMF and the World Bank. At the end of 1996, total Ukrainian debt amounted to only $8.5 billion, while the upper limit of Ukraine's debt is estimated at $15-20 billion. For the last two years we have had no problems paying our debt, including payments for oil and gas supplies from Russia and Turkmenistan. Our debt to them is respectively $3.6 billion and $2.17 billion, with an additional $704 million owed to international finance organizations.

As a result of macroeconomic progress, Ukraine is continuously increasing its foreign trade. Last year our foreign trade turnover reached $38 billion; that is, 20% more than in 1995. On the other hand, the trade deficit is shrinking and in 1996 it was only $809 million (in 1995, $1.2 billion).

We have also been able to attract a growing amount of foreign investments. In per capita terms, it is still one of the lowest in Central and Eastern Europe, but the trend is encouraging. In 1993, total foreign investment in Ukraine was $180 million; in 1994, it was $366 million; in 1995, $750 million; in 1996 it exceeded $1.5 billion. Twenty percent of all direct investment has come from the United States.

The president and government of Ukraine consider the attraction of foreign investment as the top priority of our economic policy. In the

---

[1]   By the end of 1997 the annual rate of inflation decreased to 9.2%.—Yu.S.

words of President Kuchma, 1996 was a year of unrealized opportunities. We will work hard to make this year different, to make it a year of
real breakthrough. At the end of 1996, the government submitted to the
parliament a legislative package designed to speed up the restructuring
of the Ukrainian economy, promote foreign investment, and introduce
a tax reform which would reduce the overall tax burden on domestic
and foreign investors, as well as improve the governmental mechanism
of business registration and license issuing.

To ensure the irreversible character of our reforms, Ukraine must see
economic improvement in 1997. The government's goal is to help to
create a middle class, a class of owners in business and agriculture. We
clearly understand that this is a historical challenge, and that foreign
investment will play a key role in meeting this challenge.

Let me draw your attention to the development of the U.S.-Ukrainian
relations which last year led to the establishment of U.S.-Ukrainian Binational Kuchma-Gore Commission, and to the proclamation of a strategic partnership between our two countries. The working group met in
October 1996 and established four joint committees, including committees on foreign policy, security issues, sustainable economic cooperation, and trade and investments. The commission is viewed by the two
sides as a valuable mechanism for the practical realization of their strategic partnership, and for dialogue on a broad range of bilateral and multilateral issues. So far, meetings of the three committees have been held.
The November 6, 1996 Joint statement of the Foreign Policy Committee
which took place in Washington, DC stipulates that "the U.S. and
Ukraine strategic partnership is based on common values and goals."
Even a few months ago we would not have believed such a formula to be
possible.

We are now working on the agenda for a high-level meeting of the
Binational Commission with the participation of the President of
Ukraine Leonid Kuchma and U.S. Vice President Al Gore, probably in
March or April.

I am also glad to inform you that a meeting of the Executive Board of
the Bilateral Committee on Trade and Investment in the framework of
Kuchma-Gore Commission took place in Kyiv in January of this year.

The American side has agreed to immediately renew discussion of the
issues which will greatly enhance our business relationship. They include the following:

1. Securing Ukraine's status in U.S. legislation as an "economy in transition," which is of undoubted importance for my country.

2. Ratification by the U.S. of the Bilateral Convention on Avoidance of Double Taxation. As we were informed, this Convention was approved by the U.S. Congress last summer, but was not enacted by President Clinton.

3. Extending the effect of the U.S. Generalized System of Preferences to merchandise of Ukrainian origin, which is in high demand.

4. Granting of the U.S. to Ukraine a "permanent most-favored-nation status" in trade.

5. American political support and technical assistance in the process of Ukraine's accession to the World Trade Organization.

6. Other issues that could actually boost our cooperation.

Does all that I have said tonight mean that everything is positive in our development? Of course not. No one should forget the difficult heritage our nation has inherited from more than seventy years of Communist dictatorship and a lack of democratic legal mechanisms. This adversely affected our national self-image and government. During the transformation period from the command system to a free market economy, crime and corruption have considerably increased. Recently, a number of publications in the American press focused on these and other problems which to some extent irritate Ukrainian-American relations. These problems are:

Lack of legislative action to promote a positive investment climate, high taxes, and other economic difficulties.

In this connection a number of American companies have stated their possible decisions to close their business in Ukraine. I very much believe that the adoption of the new legislative package, which I mentioned before, on tax reduction and promotion of foreign investment,s will considerably change the investment climate in 1997. This year, we hope, will be the year of foreign investments in Ukraine.

Corruption and threats against foreign businessmen.

We very carefully investigate all cases of corruption and threats to Ameri-

can businessmen and inform the Ukrainian leadership of every signal from Capitol Hill. These problems just a few days ago were discussed by President Leonid Kuchma and President of the World Bank James Wolfenson. President Kuchma reconfirmed that Operation Clean Hands, designed to combat corruption on the highest levels of our administration, will be initiated shortly. Our government will also create special groups to work with strategic investors to resolve promptly all problems.

Yesterday I had the honor and real pleasure of witnessing a significant political event of your country—the State of the Union Address to the U.S. Congress by President Bill Clinton. While listening to the President's statement, I was also thinking about the fate of my country. What will the next century bring to us Ukrainians? Mostly it depends on us, on the will of our people and their own efforts. But at the same time it also depends on our strategic partnership with the United States. Only together can we change my country's destiny and transform it into a democratic, prosperous, independent nation: an indivisible part of the Central and Eastern European region, which completely corresponds to the American strategic efforts.

Let us join our efforts.

NINE

Agribusiness, Ukraine, and the BSEC: Problems and Prospects*

Ukraine is strongly involved in the expansion of the Black Sea Economic Cooperation (BSEC). Ukraine recently reached agreements with Azerbaijan and Georgia on its participation in the construction of the Caucasian corridor for transportation of oil and other goods from Asia to Europe. Ukraine is now opening a new ferry line, "Odesa-Poti, Georgia," which can be used as an important part of that corridor. We also support the construction of a pipeline from Azerbaijan through Georgia to the Black Sea coast. Some arrangements have also been made for Ukraine's participation in the construction of the Ceyhan-Samsun pipeline on Turkish territory.

Let me cite a few general facts and figures about the agricultural potential of my country and the present course of economic reforms. Ukraine, as a 52 million-strong nation (about 16 million live in rural areas) and the second-largest country in Europe (after the European part of Russia), holds a strategic place in the Central and Eastern European region, and its strategic importance has been recognized by the U.S. and European countries. It is also very rich in various mineral resources. But its main treasure is its fertile soils, the so-called "black soils" (*chornozem*) which, in combination with its moderate climate, make Ukraine a great agricultural nation, which, before World War I, was known as the "breadbasket of Europe." We strongly believe that Ukraine has the potential to regain this important position. A positive indication of this potential is that in 1995 Ukraine began once again to export grain, after 70 years of obstruction of that potential.

Total arable land in Ukraine is approximately 83 million acres. Ukraine has 27% of the world's "black soils." The average area under

---

*   Remarks at the Black Sea Economic Community Agribusiness Council Business Luncheon (Washington, DC, February 18, 1997).

cultivation is 30 to 35 million acres, the greater part of which is under winter and spring wheat crops (13 to 15 million acres).

Another of Ukraine's important agricultural products is sugar beets. Sugar beet area now comprises between 2.5 and 3 million acres. Sunflower cultivation occupies 3.5 million acres, with the same amount of land dedicated to hay production. There are also 10 million acres of corn crops for silage and green forage. Even now, under the current severe economic crisis, Ukraine exports 1 million tons of grain, 1.5 million tons of sugar, and 0.5 million tons of sunflower seeds. Ukraine has more than 1.4 million acres of orchards and 0.3 million acres of vineyards.

Ukraine also has developed animal husbandry. The total number of cattle is approximately 20 million head, including 7.8 million cows, as well as 14 million pigs, 5.5 million sheep, and 186 million poultry. Average annual production of milk is 15 to 16 million tons; red and white meat, 3.0 to 3.2 million tons; eggs, upwards of 700 million dozen; wool, upwards of 8.0 thousand tons.

Unfortunately, Ukraine is now living through a very painful but unavoidable transitional period from a command economy to a free market. The crop in 1996 was 26.5 million metric tons, our lowest indicator for the past 40 years. This decrease was a result of severe weather conditions, reduction of planting area, and lack of fertilizers, as well as bad technical support and agricultural equipment. On the other hand, we must admit that reforms in our agricultural sector had a late start and were not as effective as in the industrial area, in which we have achieved substantial progress.[1]

Ukraine's agroindustry currently consists of about 7,600 enterprises, of which 2,500 are processing enterprises, including 192 sugar refineries, 157 flour mills, 722 soft drink plants, 104 meat plants, and 452 dairy enterprises. In the nation's economy, agroindustry accounts for about 14% of the total industrial production, and about 12% of total employment.

Today Ukraine's agriculture is undergoing reformation. There are 10,500 collective farms being reformed. The property of these farms has

---

[1] The outlook for crops this year (1997) is 35 to 36 million metric tons of grain, including 17 to 18 million metric tons of the winter and spring wheat, and sugar production is 2.2 million metric tons.—Yu.S.

been divided among collective farmers, and there have been new cooperative agricultural farms established, as well as more than 1,100 varied unions, cooperatives and other forms of property farms created.

The Ministry of the Agro-industrial Complex of Ukraine supervises more than 6,000 state enterprises (processing, building, service, etc.) and about 3,000 non-state enterprise, of which more than 80% have become private or cooperative-owned. Recently, a new list of more than 2,000 enterprises (first of all mills and elevators) for privatization has also been adopted .

Within the last six years about 35,500 private farms have been established in Ukraine. These farms extend over more than 2.2 million acres of land, and have 30,000 head of cattle, 40,000 pigs, and also sheep and poultry. There are 11.5 million plots around houses in rural Ukraine as well. Last year, private farmers and holders of small plots produced 96% of the national output in potatoes, 73% of vegetables, and more than 50% of milk and meat production. In other words the average production of agricultural commodities by private holders is 51% of all production of these goods in Ukraine in comparison to 27% five to six years ago.

The Government Program plans to transform state land into the private property of 13.6 million people living in the agricultural sector. At this time the government has already transfered 67.4 million acres of land to agricultural producers absolutely free. By the end of this year this area will have increased up to 85.1 million acres, or an increase of almost twenty million acres. The total cost of this land is 40 billion hryvnyas or $21 billion. 5.1 million people have already received certificates for land, and 70.3% of Ukrainian citizens have privatized their plots of land.

About one-third of all the fixed production assets of the country are in the agricultural sector. If one compared the economic productivity of these assets, agriculture would rank even higher—upwards of 50%. Agriculture employees, about one-fourth of the working population, contribute one-third of gross outputs and provides 70% of retail commodity turnover. Yet, Ukraine produces less than one-fourth of its true potential today. Incredibly, today, food security is an issue in Ukraine, one of the world's potentially most productive breadbaskets.

With relatively modest investments in infrastructure and technology and with real substantive reform in government policy, our agriculture can become an enormous generator of wealth, jobs, and opportunity.

And importantly for us, the returns on investments and in production in our agriculture sector are only a crop cycle away. As President Kuchma said, "The Agroindustrial sector should take the lead in the process of overcoming economic crisis."

At present, Ukraine represents a huge market opportunity for a wide array of goods, services and capital. According to an evaluation by the Citizen Network for Foreign Affairs, a U.S. non-profit organization, Ukraine needs the following:

1. The establishment of modern information networks for producers regarding market situations and advanced technologies.

2. The formation of a system of wholesale agricultural markets, commodity exchanges, and a futures trading system.

3. The institutionalization of small and large private business, intermediary, trading, and manufacturing companies.

4. The technical modernization of Ukraine's agriculture, introducing advanced technologies and new, highly effective agricultural machinery.

5. The modernization of seed production, cattle breeding, introduction of new highly productive agricultural plants and cattle breeds, and improvement in systems of poultry and fish-breeding.

6. The use and production of highly effective pesticides, herbicides, fertilizers, and premixes.

7. The creation of the agricultural processing infrastructure, transportation, and storage and preservation of agricultural products to reduce losses of yield.

8. The modernization of the packing industry.

9. Solving energy and environmental problems of the agricultural sector.

10. Participation in modernizing the construction industry for building enterprises and private housing.

The annual market requirements for primary agricultural inputs— that is, crop protection products, fertilizers, equipment etc.—is estimated to be upwards of $6 billion. Today that market is somewhere around $300–$350 million.

One last fact. The annual replacement requirements for harvesters for the next 10 to 15 years is estimated to be between six and eight thousand combines. Indeed an estimated 40% of the current fleet of 85,000 combines is considered worn out and needs to be replaced immediately.

There is a very good example of the cooperation between two countries that I would like to mention. I have in mind specifically the cooperation between Ukraine and the United States. During the past five years of Ukraine's independence we have established very close ties with the U.S. not only in the political arena and in military operation, but first of all in the field of economics. Our ties with the Department of Agriculture have been very productive and the technical assistance we have received has been extremely worthwhile in the training and development of more than 300 of our citizens, who have learned the mechanics of the free enterprise system and about the organization of agricultural production. As well the extension of about $100 million in credits has been vital for the purchase of goods needed for our agricultural production. We are very grateful to the Agriculture Department's administration for the assistance given us.

The U.S. government has opened for Ukraine other credit lines. One of them is the short term credit line for $175 million to purchase oil, herbicides, and pesticides and components of these materials to produce them in Ukraine. We have received also medium term credit line for $250 million dollars. Ukraine has already bought 1,049 John Deere and 400 Case combines. The capacity of these American combines is up to three times higher than that of the Russian "Don" combine, and up to eight times higher than the Russian "Niva" combine. Recently the Kherson Combine Plant and Deere & Company announced that they are creating a joint venture company to produce this type of combine in Ukraine.

Due to grants from the USAID and USIA more than 300 teachers and undergraduates have visited American universities. Last year Ukraine's National Agrarian University and Iowa State University signed a special memorandum providing for the recognition of their courses, grades, and certificates and diplomas as equivalent. Thanks to our cooperation with Iowa State University and the World Bank the National Agrarian University has established an Agribusiness Institute which also includes a School of Foreign Economic Affairs.

A number of well-known companies such as "Monsanto," "Cargill," "John Deere," "Case," "Kyiv-Atlantic," and others, are participating in intensive efforts to restore Ukraine's agriculture sector back to its previous glorious reputation as the breadbasket of Europe. Many of these American companies came to Ukraine due to efforts of the Citizen Network for Foreign Affairs (CNFA) for the implementation of practical projects, which are now helping to harvest grain on 200 thousand hectares.

The U.S. government gave these companies a grant of over 10 million dollars through CNFA to help reconstruct our agriculture. And companies have invested into these projects $60 million of their own money besides. "Cargill" signed an agreement last year to build in Ukraine a sunflower processing plant with a capacity of 300 thousand metric tons per year.

CNFA created the Ukrainian Agricultural Development Company (UADC)—a highly innovative, structured trade finance company. UADC is owned by nine major Western agriculture input suppliers and backed by a syndication of leading European banks. Organized as a for-profit corporation, UADC and its banking coalition will provide $50 million of advance payments against commodities for the 1997 crop year to purchase critically needed farm inputs. The advance payments will be structured on a shared-risk basis, with the participating banks and agribusiness sharing the risk. Over the next three years UADC aims to provide $300 million in advance payment against commodities to an expanding network of our private farm supply enterprises.

Speaking about prospects of agribusiness in Ukraine, we proceed from the fact that the future of the entire economic reform in Ukraine depends on progress in the agricultural sector. In other words, revitalization of our agriculture means the revitalization of Ukraine.

TEN

Ukraine and NATO Enlargement*

I would like to draw your attention to the problem of NATO enlargement. This issue has recently moved from the sphere of discussion and hypothetical statement to that of concrete political decision. In his speech in Detroit on October 22, 1996, President Clinton clearly formulated the goal of the United States: in 1999, in connection with the fiftieth anniversary of the Alliance, and ten years after the fall of the "Berlin wall," the first group of countries will become full-fledged NATO members.

NATO Ministerials of December 1996 supported this proposal and decided that at the Madrid Summit of Alliance in July, 1997 an invitation will be sent to one or several countries to join NATO, and respective negotiations will begin.

The issue of NATO enlargement has recently become the focus of attention of the Ukrainian leadership, which attaches the greatest importance to it. The analysis of Ukrainian experts, in particular those from the National Security and Defense Council, testify that most probably the countries of the first tranche to enter NATO will include Poland, the Czech Republic, and Hungary. In this case Ukraine will have a common border with NATO stretching for 330 miles. If Slovakia and Romania are added to the process, the common border with NATO will have a length of 563 miles. Understandably, this will mean a sharp change in the geostrategic situation, not only of Ukraine, but of Europe at large.

In 1996 and the beginning of 1997, the question of NATO enlargement became the subject of numerous speeches by President Leonid Kuchma, National Security and Defense Council Secretary Volodymyr Horbulin, Minister of Foreign Affairs Hennadiy Udovenko, and other

---

* Remarks delivered at the National Defense University (Washington, DC, March 4, 1997).

officials. During the talks in the autumn of last year in Washington, these issues were also the focus of intensive consideration for U.S. National Security Advisor Anthony Lake, Secretary of State Warren Christopher, Deputy Secretary of State Strobe Talbott, Defense Secretary William Perry, and other U.S. administration representatives.

Ukraine's stand on the issue of NATO enlargement is consistent, widely known, and very transparent:

1. Ukraine regards NATO as an alliance of democratic peace-loving countries, and one of the most effective structures for stability and security in the Euro-Atlantic region. Important for Ukraine is not only the defense organization of NATO, but also the political structures which foster the development of science and technology, information, and medical and humanitarian ties.

In the NATO-Ukraine Joint Press Statement of September 14, 1995, it was stated that:

> The Ukrainian side highly appreciated the process of NATO's continuing and active adaptation to meet the changing circumstances of the Euro-Atlantic security. It was stressed that NATO played a vital role in the dialogue on political, military and security issues aimed at promoting a general climate of confidence in the Euro-Atlantic area. In promoting this climate, it was noted that special attention should be paid to strict respect for territorial integrity, existing borders, and rights of persons belonging to national minorities. Both sides shared the view that NATO enlargement should be directed at enhancing security of all countries in Europe without creating dividing lines and taking into account political and security developments in the whole of Europe. Both sides also agreed that the further development of NATO-Ukraine relations will contribute to enhancing European security.

2. Ukraine does not oppose the expansion of NATO, because that is an objective process. We see the future of NATO as the gradual transformation of a predominantly defensive bloc into a Euro-Atlantic security structure for all European states. Ukraine does not consider NATO a potential enemy or threat to its interests. As the Ukrainian minister of defense declared, Ukraine will not move additional forces towards its western borders when NATO is enlarged eastward. The decision to enter military-political structures, including NATO, is the right of any

nation, and no "third party" has the "veto" power over this decision.

3. To avoid new division lines in Europe, the principle of indivisibility of security should be observed. The primary national security interests of all interest nations, including non-bloc and neutral states, should thus be ensured. Ukraine is no exception. Its place in Europe, Ukraine's non-bloc policy—directed at the prevention of the reappearance of bloc confrontation—demands that our interests be taken into consideration as fully as possible. NATO expansion should be a gradual, evolutionary, transparent, process and not a revolutionary action.

4. Ukraine was seriously concerned over the possibility of stationing nuclear weapons on the territory of new member-states, and by territorial claims from certain candidates. Ukraine could not agree with even the theoretical possibility of the stationing of tactical nuclear weapons on the territory of neighboring countries, when Ukraine had, as early as 1992, voluntarily withdrawn the tactical nuclear arms located on its own territory. Trying to avoid the return to Cold War confrontational times, President of Ukraine Leonid Kuchma proposed the establishment of a nuclear-free zone in Central and Eastern Europe from the Black Sea to the Baltic Sea, fully capitalizing on the shrinking of the area where nuclear weapons were deployed, because of the withdrawal of such weapons from Ukraine. This is why we commend the declaration by the December 1996 NATO Ministerials that NATO has no plans, no intentions, and no reason to station nuclear weapons on the territory of future new member-states. Ukraine held intensive negotiations in the subject with NATO and its individual members, and is satisfied that Ukraine's stand was fully taken into account by the Alliance.

5. Ukraine, which at present is the largest non-bloc country of Europe, will not necessarily retain its non-bloc status in the future. At the present, Ukraine does not want to join any military bloc (Tashkent or NATO). At the same time, as was stressed by Mr. Horbulin, secretary of the National Security and Defense Council of Ukraine, after his visit to Brussels last January, "today we are not yet ready [to join NATO] but we do not exclude such a possibility." We can raise the issue of joining NATO at an appropriate time. However, Ukraine is not now ready to meet all the requirements put forward to candidates for NATO membership. If we have made significant progress with respect to such political requirements as the establishment of a democratic society, civil

control of the military, good neighborly relations with adjacent countries, etc., we still have much to do to meet the approximately 1,800 technical requirements and criteria necessary for full-fledged membership in NATO.

By the way, according to a recent opinion poll, 36% of Ukrainians support the idea of joining NATO (15% think it should be done as soon as possible; 21%, sometime later), and only 19% are against the move, while 45% remain undecided. It is worthwhile to bear in mind that, in December 1994, only 9% supported Ukraine's accession to NATO.

"The Conception of National Security of Ukraine," which was adopted by the Parliament of Ukraine on January 16, 1997, defines as one of the principle tasks of the state policy in the field of national security, "participation in universal and regional security systems which exist already or are being established." Ukraine, actively expanding its "enhanced relationship" with NATO within the framework of the North Atlantic Cooperation Council (NACC), the Partnership for Peace (PfP) Program, and beyond, hopes to establish a special partnership with the Alliance, which should result in the conclusion of a relevant document. We think that the process of political and military collaboration between NATO and Ukraine should not be linked with the development of relations between NATO and Russia. These two parallel activities should be pursued separately and independently. We hope that in the spring we will reach an understanding with the Alliance on the substance of a NATO-Ukraine document on our special relationship.

The December 1996 NATO Ministerial Meeting acknowledged that the maintenance of Ukraine's independence, territorial integrity and sovereignty is crucial to stability and security in Europe. It was recognized that Ukraine's development of a strong, enduring relationship with NATO is an important aspect of the emerging European security architecture. NATO foreign ministers greatly valued the active participation of Ukraine in the Partnership for Peace.

I want to remind you that cooperation within the PfP framework envisages the attainment of the following goals:

1. Promoting openness in national defense planning and forming the defense budget.

2. Providing democratic control over armed forces.

3. Maintaining the option and readiness to participate in the operations

conducted under the UN auspices and/or within OSCE responsibility, within the limits allowed by the Constitution.

4. Developing cooperative relations with NATO in the defense sphere with the aim of joint planning and military training and exercises meant to raise their capability to fulfill tasks connected with peace-keeping activities, search and rescue operations, operations to provide humanitarian aid, and other goals which can soon be agreed upon.

5. Forming, in the long run, such armed forces as can better interact with the armed forces of NATO states.

The final stage of our joining the PfP is the preparation and conclusion of the individual partnership program between Ukraine and NATO, which stipulates concrete measures and actions in which Ukraine will participate.

During 1996, Ukraine took part in over 150 activities within the framework of PfP, including 17 military exercises. In 1997, the Ukrainian Armed Forces plans to take part in over 200 activities under this program. In June 1996, for the first time on Ukrainian territory, the PfP exercises under the name "Peace Shield-96" took place, involving troops from Ukraine, the United States, Russia, Poland, Hungary, Slovakia, and other participants. In August 1996, a marine platoon from Ukraine took part in the exercises "Cooperative Osprey-96" on the territory of the United States. As a result of the exercises, this platoon finished the exercise first among 16 participating units. Secretary William Perry and Atlantic Command Chief General John J. Sheehan noted the excellent preparation of the Ukrainian platoon. In 1997, on the territory of Ukraine, is planned the "Cooperative Neighbor-97" exercise, to which we plan to invite high-level chiefs of staff.

In general, the Ukrainian Armed Forces, in cooperation with the armed forces of 31 countries, concluded 127 bilateral agreements in the field of military and defense cooperation.

To provide for regional stability and security during the first stage of NATO enlargement, and to avoid new division lines and confrontations in Europe, we consider it necessary to:

1. Guarantee the openness of NATO in the future under the slogan "NATO's doors should not be closed to anyone."

2. Complement the process of NATO enlargement by deepening its cooperation with other structures and with all interested states of the region; that is, the alliance should be transformed in the direction of a structure for collective security, as has recently been stated by Secretary of State Warren Christopher during his trip to Germany.

3. Proceeding from the principle of indivisibility of security, to take into account the interests and concerns of all countries of the region. During the NATO enlargement, Ukraine's security interests should be taken into account. For Ukraine in this context, the following provisions matter most:

> a. Assurance that none of the member states lay any territorial claims against Ukraine.
> b. Non-deployment of nuclear weapons in the territory of new member-states.
> c. Establishment of a special partnership between Ukraine and NATO by the conclusion of a special bilateral document.

If the second of the above-mentioned issues can already be considered solved, the other two, as I mentioned, still require further consultations.

On the first issue we have the reassuring statement by the NATO ministers of foreign affairs that, "the maintenance of Ukraine's independence, territorial integrity and sovereignty is a crucial factor for stability and security in Europe."

On the third point, Ukraine has already submitted to NATO members its vision of a possible special partnership with the Alliance, and has submitted a Ukrainian draft of a possible document on this subject. Respective consultations are being carried out now, and we hope that the document will be ready for signature by the NATO Summit in Madrid.

Let me also draw your attention to the official visit of NATO Secretary General Mr. Javier Solana to Kyiv April 15–16, 1996. During this visit, the main topics discussed embraced included: First, further enhancement of cooperation between NATO and Ukraine, and elaboration of certain mechanisms for the implementation of the enhanced Ukraine-NATO relationship beyond the Partnership for Peace program and NACC activities. Second, regional security in Central and Eastern

European countries and on the terrain of the former USSR, with consideration of possible NATO enlargement. And, third, prospects for the establishment of the NATO Information Center in Kyiv.

The Ukrainian side stressed that it is interested in further developing active cooperation with the North Atlantic Alliance, both within the framework of the NACC activities and the PfP program, and in a wider format. Furthermore, Ukraine expressed its readiness to conclude a separate politically and legally binding agreement on special partnership relations between Ukraine and NATO. It was stated also that for the time being the issue of Ukraine's accession to NATO is not on the agenda, though the non-aligned status of Ukraine should not be an obstacle to the comprehensive strengthening of Ukraine-NATO relations in various fields.

The Ukrainian side upheld that it neither opposes the idea of NATO enlargement on principle, nor considers it a threat to national security. At the same time, Ukraine believes that, while implementing this idea, our security interests must absolutely be taken into consideration. The whole process of NATO enlargement should be gradual, evolutionary, and transparent.

The Secretary General was informed about the activities taking place in Ukraine for establishing an Interagency Working Group on the coordination of Ukraine's participation in the PfP. Members of the NATO delegation met with the leadership of the Ukrainian Institute of International Relations, which has been suggested as a site for the NATO Information Center in Kyiv.

The Secretary General underscored the exceptional importance of further strengthening of the Ukraine-NATO relationship as one of the key factors promoting stability and security in Europe. According to Mr. Solana, all Allies share the conviction that consolidation of an independent, stable and economically viable Ukraine is nowadays a crucial factor for strengthening European security.

The Secretary General expressed his gratitude to the Government of Ukraine for its active participation in NATO-led IFOR operations in Bosnia and Herzegovina, as well as in the UN operation in Eastern Slavonia.

The Secretary General underlined the interests of NATO in comprehensive broadening cooperation with Ukraine, particularly in civil emergency planning, scientific, technological, and military fields.

The Secretary General expressed his understanding of Ukraine's position on NATO enlargement and concerns regarding the possible deployment of nuclear weapons on the territory of new member-states, as well as respective reorientation of its military infrastructure. Mr. Solana declared that the issue of the deployment of nuclear weapons on the territory of new NATO member-states "is not on the agenda."

Both parties agreed that Ukraine-NATO political dialogue, including within the "16+1" format, is to become permanent and regular.

Also we consider very important the latest meeting of the American-Ukrainian Advisory Committee led by Zbigniew Brzezinski and First Deputy Minister of Ukraine Anton Buteiko with the participation of several prominent politicians from both sides. The meeting was held in Kyiv on October 10–11, 1996. Among the committee's recommendations were the following:

1. To urge NATO leaders to invite Ukraine to participate in the forthcoming NATO summit on Alliance enlargement.

2. To urge the Ukrainian government and parliament to formulate a clear policy position concerning Kyiv's policy toward NATO in the short, mid, and long terms. Ukraine's position and role as a "non-aligned" or "neutral" state should be clarified. In determining its future course, Ukraine should possess full freedom of choice.

3. To encourage and help Ukraine enhance its cooperation within the Partnership for Peace program and beyond (16+1), in various spheres (military, political, environmental, nuclear non-proliferation, etc.). A bilateral document laying down the principles for this special form of cooperation should be formulated.

4. To urge the Ukrainian government to develop closer relations with individual NATO members (including possible security agreement), and not only with NATO as an institution. For example, the ministerial level bilateral working groups between the U.S. and Ukraine can be expanded to deal with security-related issues such as energy, the environment, and Ukrainian ties with Western and Central Europe.

5. To urge the U.S. government to facilitate early realization of the North Atlantic Council's ministerial decision to establish a NATO information office in Kyiv to better inform military personnel and ordinary civilians about the mission and operations of the Atlantic Alliance.

6. To urge closer cooperation between Ukraine and the West European Union (WEU) through bilateral multilateral arrangements and participation in a range of WEU programs. The WEU must promptly provide Ukraine with associate partnership status.

While expanding our partnership with NATO we also understand that it is still necessary to do much to consolidate Ukrainian society, reorienting its priorities with the aim of strengthening ties with trans-European structures, first transforming our economy and integrating it into the world market system.

An important element of Ukraine's strategy toward NATO is our interest in the development of equal and mutually advantageous ties with our largest neighbor, Russia, and in the development of a constructive cooperation between NATO and Russia.

The above-mentioned facts and reflections testify to the following:

Within the last year the position of Ukraine has further developed in favor of strengthening cooperation between Ukraine and NATO.

Ukraine will continue to secure its national interests by strongly opposing NATO membership for countries which have territorial claims against Ukraine.

Ukraine highly appreciates actions made by NATO to take into account our position regarding non-deployment of nuclear weapons on the territory of new member states. We consider this move to be eloquent evidence of enhanced cooperation between Ukraine and the Alliance.

Ukraine is looking forward to the conclusion of an agreement on special relations with NATO, which would envisage closer collaboration with the Alliance in political, defense, economic, and military-technical spheres, in the areas of science, technology and the environment, dealing with emergency situations, the information sphere, etc. As I already mentioned, Ukraine has submitted a draft agreement on the special relations with NATO for appropriate consideration.

Eleven

The Geopolitical Situation of Ukraine at Present and in the Future*

Several fundamental features of the current geopolitical situation in which Ukraine finds itself are going to play an important long-term role in the 21st century. First, simultaneous disintegration and integration processes are continuing on the territory of the former USSR, disintegration being dominant. At least six geostrategic regions have emerged as a result, embracing countries—or groups of countries—with different political systems, dissimilar economic potentials and divergent national goals: 1) Ukraine; 2) Russia and Belarus; 3) Moldova; 4) the Baltic States; 5) the Trans-Caucasus countries; 6) and the countries of Central Asia. Each region has its own conflicts and problems. Similar processes are taking place within the Russian Federation. Russia, however, is trying to lead the process of reintegration by forging alliances within the Newly Independent States (NIS): Russia-Belarus, Russia-Belarus-Kazakhstan-Kyrgyzstan, and the Tashkent military alliance.

The latest development that will be a major factor in strengthening stability in Europe is the historical Treaty of Friendship, Cooperation, and Partnership, signed by the President of Ukraine Leonid Kuchma and Russian President Boris Yeltsin in Kyiv on May 31, 1997. From now on, relations between these two independent states will be legally based on the principle of mutual respect, sovereign equality, inviolability of borders, territorial integrity, peaceful settlement of disputes, and non-use of force or threat of force. The final settlement of legal and economic issues pertaining to the status, division, and stationing of the Black Sea Fleet in the Ukrainian city of Sevastopol enhances considerably regional stability and will also influence the development of the region in the 21st century.

* An earlier version of this article was published in the *Analysis of Current Events* 9(8) August 1997.

Many other agreements significant to its geostrategic position in the post-Soviet environment were concluded by Ukraine: consolidation of the strategic partnership with Azerbaijan, Georgia, and Uzbekistan through cooperation in providing a Trans-Caucasian corridor for the transport of oil from the Caspian region to Europe over the territory of Ukraine; the participation of Ukraine (together with Russia and Moldova) in the peaceful settlement of the Transdnistrian conflict; and consolidation of ties with Estonia, Latvia, Lithuania and Poland along the Baltic Sea-Black Sea axis. On May 27, 1997, President Kuchma, together with the presidents of the three Baltic States and Poland, signed a joint communiqué, which placed special emphasis on the consolidation of efforts to create a stable, secure, integrated, and indivisible Europe where no country would be threatened by another. The presidents underscored the fact that every state has the right to choose the means and instruments to ensure its security, especially by treaties or alliances. This is one of the key principles of the Organization on Security and Cooperation in Europe (OSCE). The joint position was that NATO's doors should remain open to all states aspiring to membership. In Tallinn, where the summit took place, the leaders pledged to cooperate within the framework of the Partnership for Peace program (PfP) in order to ensure its better adjustment to the new changes and challenges in the area of security in Europe.

Second, the strategic goal of Ukraine, expressed by President Kuchma, is to integrate into European and Euro-Atlantic structures, to gradually establish a special partnership with the European Union (EU), NATO, and the WEU, and to be active in shaping a new European security structure. Ukraine, being a large European state and a natural component of the Central and Eastern European region (CEE), aimed at overcoming an imposed long-standing alienation from the other nations of Europe. While taking into account the economic advantages of integration into Europe, Ukraine regards cooperation with NATO, the EU, and the CEE countries as a priority component of its national security.

The development of regional cooperation is also an important stabilizing factor. Ukraine pays great attention to relations with neighboring states of Central and Eastern Europe—Poland, Romania, Hungary and Slovakia. It has recently become a full member of the Central European Initiative and considers it to be the beginning of development in large-scale regional cooperation. Interested in moving further, Ukraine is seeking, in particular, accession to the Central European Free Trade Agreement.

Ukraine favors a broad approach to European security that covers not only military, but also political, ethnic, economic, and ecological aspects. Such an approach should support the development of democratic processes in the region and the establishment of mutually beneficial friendly relations among states. A necessary element in this new security is a collective capability to deal with new challenges or threats, such as the proliferation of weapons of mass destruction, drug trafficking, international terrorism, organized crime, and illegal migration. Recognizing the indivisibility and comprehensive nature of European security, Ukrainian security policy is based on this principle.

Third, a fundamental factor determining the geopolitical situation of Ukraine is the recent decision on NATO enlargement. After Poland and Hungary join NATO in 1999, Ukraine will have several hundred miles of common border with NATO. Clearly, this would mean a sharp change in the geostrategic situation not only of Ukraine, but of Europe at large. Talks about NATO expansion and about the language of the Ukraine-NATO document were intensified in Washington and in Brussels during 1997.

The enlargement of NATO up to the territory of Ukraine will play a positive stabilizing role, as Ukraine has strategic partnership relations with Poland, a treaty with Romania, signed in June 1997, and good neighborly relations with Slovakia and Hungary. During the last two years, the Ukrainian leadership and the Ministry of Foreign Affairs have been persistently striving for Ukraine's interests to be taken into account and for the establishment of special partnership with NATO. The path to the "Charter on a Distinctive Partnership Between Ukraine and The North Atlantic Treaty Organization" was not simple. The Charter was signed on July 9, 1997, in Madrid, by the president of Ukraine, Leonid Kuchma, NATO Secretary General Javier Solana and leaders of all 16 countries—member of NATO, including President Clinton of the United States. As a member of the official Ukrainian delegation to Madrid, I was happy to be an eyewitness to this solemn historical event, which will play an important role in the fate of Ukraine in the 21st century. The Ukraine-NATO Charter contains five parts: 1) Building an enhanced Ukraine-NATO Relationship; 2) Principles for the Development of Ukraine-NATO Relations; 3) Area for Consultation and/or Cooperation Between Ukraine and NATO; 4) Practical Arrangements for Consultation and Cooperation Between Ukraine and NATO; and 5) Cooperation for a More Secure Europe. Given the importance of informational activities to improve mutual knowledge and understanding, NATO has also established an Information and Documentation Center in Kyiv.

Ukraine and NATO consider their relationship as an evolving, dynamic process. The Ukraine-NATO Commission will meet, as a rule, not less than twice a year. Ukraine has received security assurances from all five nuclear-weapon state-parties to the Nuclear Non-proliferation Treaty (NPT) as a non-nuclear weapon state-party to NPT. Ukraine welcomes the statement by NATO members that "enlarging the Alliance will not require a change in NATO's current nuclear posture and, therefore, NATO countries have no intention, no plan, and no reason to deploy nuclear weapons on the territory of new members."

The most important step for Ukraine now is to implement the provisions of this Charter—a treaty that will have geostrategic significance in the future. Predicting the future of Ukraine after the NATO enlargement must take into account three major factors:

(1) *The position of the United States of America.* By establishing relations of Strategic Partnership with Ukraine, the United States has demonstrated its profound understanding of the key role that Ukraine plays in the system of European security. Further developments in this sensitive and extremely important region will depend to a great extent on the United States and its consistency in supporting Ukraine. We hope that the United States in the future will not support the creation of new spheres of influence in the region, but rather will pursue a balanced policy of equal partnership, taking into consideration the national interests of all countries in this part of Europe.

(2) *Russia's Position.* There is a unique consensus in the present-day Russia among the major political forces, ranging from modern pro-western democratic reformers to aggressive nationalist radicals. Lamentation over the lost grandeur of Russia, embodied in the former Soviet Empire, makes up the core of this consensus. Russia will have to make a dramatic choice in the 21st century: either to become a democratic country on the European model with a prosperous market economy

and friendly relations with its neighbors on the basis of acknowledging their sovereignty and independence—and we hope this will be the way of Russia's development—or to try to create a new empire, which is impossible without incorporating Ukraine. The pattern of political and economic development of the Russian state in the near future is going to dictate the "rules of the game" for its neighboring countries, including Ukraine. Any attempts to restore the empire or to forcefully reintegrate the post-Soviet countries under Russian control will accelerate the movement of Ukraine toward NATO.

(3) *Policies and Developments in Ukraine.* This is perhaps the most crucial factor. The geostrategic place of Ukraine in the future depends on its economic development, success in the carrying out reforms, and the recovery of industrial and agricultural potential on market-based principles. This should provide for a consistent growth of GDP and welfare of the people. If the Ukrainian economy weakens and its economic policies fail, Ukraine's independence will face a difficult test. Access to Europe will be blocked by the European Union and NATO. Only by providing for the prosperity of Ukraine by creating a middle class of about seven to ten million private property owners, will we be able to secure Ukraine's independence and its affiliation with Europe in the 21st century.

From Chornobyl to Madrid

While working on the present volume, I have thought about the last eleven years, from 1986 to 1997, which have played a critical role in the history of Ukraine in the twentieth century and completely changed the destiny of Ukraine, not to mention my own personal fate.

As a starting point, I have taken Chornobyl in 1986—the worst technogenic catastrophe at a nuclear power plant—and what resulted from the death and suffering that my country experienced. Chornobyl also turned out to be a threatening oracle for the Soviet Empire, which went on to its own self-destruction, and in whose death throes an opportunity arose by which a sovereign Ukraine could be born and start along a democratic path without shedding blood.

After Chornobyl the Ukrainian people have their eyes wide open, understanding that it is absolutely necessary for them to build their *own* state—one that will protect them from, and not subject them to, ecological threats and other dangers. We have begun to build that state and we have found our own geopolitical place in the world. Ukraine has survived the change of its political and economic orders, the turnover in many of its leadership positions—from the aparatchik Volodymyr Shcherbytskyi, installed by the Moscow Communist Politburo, to President Leonid Kuchma, chosen by the Ukrainian electorate in free and fully democratic elections that took place in an independent and sovereign Ukraine. An extraordinarily large number of dramatic events have been compressed into a short period of time. This brief history has, in turn, completely cancelled out the stereotypes of the Soviet period.

And so, to put in two words the historical path we have traveled during these few, brief years, I would say: from Chornobyl to Madrid. To Madrid, where one sunny morning, on July 9, 1997, the president of Ukraine, Leonid Kuchma, signed the "Charter on a Distinctive NATO-Ukraine Partnership." Javier Solana and the heads of state of the sixteen NATO countries, including President Bill Clinton, also signed. At the beginning of this path one could not have envisioned where Ukraine would stand in so short a time.

Speaking during the solemn ceremony, President Kuchma said:

> Madrid in 1997 will undoubtedly go down in history as a city where a dividing line left by the Cold War in the very center of Europe has been eliminated...

> In a few minutes the charter of special cooperation between Ukraine and NATO is to be signed. This historic document is going to be one more piece of convincing evidence of the fact that on the European continent a new security architecture based on openness and partnership is being shaped...The state of Ukraine feels itself now an integral part of Central, Eastern, and Southern Europe and is ready to take part in providing peace and stability in these regions and in the continent in general.[1]

In his speech, President Clinton underscored the fact that:

> Today we take another step toward that new Europe with the signing of this Charter between a new NATO and a democratic Ukraine... This Charter launches a closer relationship between NATO and Ukraine that will benefit both. It lays a foundation for consultation and cooperation. It welcomes Ukraine as our partner in building an undivided Europe...Ukraine has emerged from a century of struggle to pursue the highest standards of dignity and freedom. It is tackling tough economic reform. It has been a leader in reducing the nuclear danger...

> Today, Europe's security is not a matter of competition but of cooperation on behalf of common goals. It is natural for Ukraine to reach out to NATO and for NATO to do the same, helping to secure Ukraine firmly in the heart of a new and undivided democratic Europe.[2]

The signing of this charter brought Ukraine firmly into the fold of those countries that have made a decisive step along the path toward integration into Euro-Atlantic structures—back toward Europe after a

---

[1] *Remarks by President Clinton, Prime Minister of Spain Aznar, Secretary General of NATO Solana and President Kuchma of Ukraine in Signing Ceremony of NATO-Ukraine Charter.* The White House, Office of the Press Secretary. Palacio Municipal de Congresos. Madrid, 9 July 1997.

[2] Ibid.

century of provincial, semi-colonial existence. In Madrid, Ukraine received, if not *de jure,* then *de facto* recognition as a country that is a part of *both* Central and Eastern Europe. Ukraine's unprecedented foreign policy successes during the period from April to July of 1997, crowned by the ceremony for the signing of the Charter in Madrid, have created a qualitatively new geopolitical situation in Europe, recognizing the key role that Ukraine plays in general European security on the threshold of the twenty-first century.

Among the most important of those new strategic elements that Ukraine's independent and consistent foreign policy has brought forward to the world stage, I would name the following:

> 1. Ukraine, as a non-nuclear power, acted to block the permanent spread of nuclear weapons into Central Europe during the enlargement of NATO.

> 2. Strengthening its partnership with NATO, Ukraine did not allow the rise of new lines of division on the continent or the appearance of "gray security zones" (*de facto* spheres of influence). This led to a fundamental strengthening of our national security in a westward direction.

> 3. Ukraine has *de facto* made impossible the rebirth of empire within the post-Soviet space and for the first time in three hundred years has broken the psychological boundaries of the former Russian imperial borders, recognizing itself as both a Central and East European country and stating as a goal its integration into Euro-Atlantic structures.

> 4. By establishing the relations of a strategic partnership with the U.S., and having signed treaties with Russia, Romania, and Poland, despite ancient mutual antagonisms, Ukraine has become a model for other newly independent states. This will have a long-standing effect in the region.

From Chornobyl to Madrid has been my personal fate. I took part in both of these historical events, writing a documentary narrative about the Chornobyl catastrophe[3] and, as the ambassador of Ukraine to the United States, closely cooperating with my American colleagues to prepare for the ceremony in Madrid. I take great pride in the fact that I was a part of the Ukrainian delegation to Madrid on July 9, 1997. The road

---

[3] Yuri Shcherbak [Iurii], *Chernobyl. A Documentary Story.* Edmonton: CIUS, 1989.—editor

from Chornobyl to Madrid led not only through Kyiv and Brussels, but also through Washington. The Ukrainian-American strategic partnership, announced at the end of 1996, was an important factor in our drawing closer to NATO and other Euro-Atlantic structures.

To underscore this point I would like to cite here the history of the preparation of the Charter, as recently set forth by the Director for Russian, Ukrainian and Eurasian Affairs of the National Security Council, Carlos Pascual:

> The path that led to the NATO-Ukraine Charter may be as important as the actual signing—both for the way in which Ukraine's interests were addressed, and the way in which it marked the practical elements of the U.S.-Ukraine strategic partnership.
>
> Work on the Charter was launched in earnest during a visit to Kiev by Deputy Secretary of State Strobe Talbott in July 1996 which included crucial talks with President Kuchma, National Security and Defense Council Secretary Horbulyn and Foreign Minister Udovenko. Several understandings were reached. For the United States, Deputy Secretary Talbott affirmed that NATO enlargement would proceed, but in a way that contributes to a secure and undivided Europe. And for this to occur, the United States was committed to ensuring that the transformation of Europe's security structures would serve Ukraine's interests, as well as the rest of Europe's. Ukraine's leaders affirmed their support for NATO enlargement and Ukraine's commitment to seek an expanded role in the new Europe and its security institutions. Noting that Ukraine was not seeking NATO membership, Ukraine's leaders indicated that another alternative was available that would link Ukraine to Europe's preeminent security institution. Hence, the rationale for the NATO-Ukraine partnership was born.
>
> The next step was to build multilateral support for a NATO-Ukraine partnership. Secretary Christopher signaled American commitment to an enhanced partnership between NATO and Ukraine in a major speech in September 1996. Also in September, Vice President Gore and President Kuchma announced the creation of the Bilateral Commission to deepen bilateral cooperation. And for the first time the term "strategic partnership" was applied to the U.S.-Ukraine relationship. The diplomatic foundations were thus laid to galvanize Western support for the negotiations between NATO and Ukraine that were to evolve over the following eight months.
>
> The Charter's substantive framework was drawn from a Ukrainian concept paper provided to the United States and other NATO allies in

October-November 1996. Bilateral discussions in Washington and other NATO capitals prompted further elaboration of Ukraine's concept paper which Ukraine formally submitted to NATO in November. Through February the United States and NATO Allies carefully reviewed Ukraine's ideas, and in March NATO provided Ukraine with the "basic elements" for a partnership document. The "basic elements" were reworked into a draft Charter that Secretary General Solana presented to President Kuchma on May 7 in Kiev. That very day Solana presided over the opening of a NATO information office in Kiev, the first anywhere in the former Soviet Union.[4]

And in this way an important and dramatic stage in Ukraine's history was completed as Ukraine went from Chornobyl and to Madrid. Today, Ukraine looks with faith and hope into the future, to the twenty-first century. What will the future hold for us Ukrainians? We have faith that Ukraine will improve its economy and social situation, it will strengthen its foreign relations position and will become a consistent and reliable strategic factor in the security of Europe and the world. Time will pass— perhaps ten or fifteen years—and some historian or politician will pen a new article entitled, "Ukraine: From Madrid to…"

No one knows the pathways of the future. But God grant that Ukraine follow the pathways of independence, rebirth, and freedom.

Yuri Shcherbak
September 20, 1997

---

[4]   Carlos Pascual. "Ukraine and its National Security." *Analysis of Current Events* 9(8) August 1997.

Chronology of Ukraine-U.S. Relations, 1989–1997*

1989

May 19, 1989: The U.S. Senate sends a protest to General Secretary Gorbachev his handling of Ukrainian national and human rights campaigners.

October, 1989: Ukrainian parliament member (MP) Volodymyr Yavorivskyi visits the U.S.

November 15, 1989: The U.S. Senate urges President Bush to pressure Gorbachev to legalize the Ukrainian churches previously banned under Soviet rule.

1990

July 16, 1990: Ukraine formally declares sovereignty within the USSR.

September 1990: Ukrainian MP and former political prisoner Mykhailo Horyn visits the U.S. where he meets with high-level diplomats, including Secretary of Defense Richard Cheney. Gorbachev and Shevardnadze had urged the Bush administration not to meet with Horyn.

December 12, 1990: Premier (Chairman of UkrSSR Council of Ministers) Vitold Fokin visits Washington. Meets with Bush's national security advisor Brent Scowcroft, Lawrence Eagleburger, and others. They discuss the social and economic situation in Ukraine as well as the course of ties between the U.S. and the UkrSSR.

1991

February 6, 1991: At a hearing of the Council for Security and Cooperation in Europe (hereafter *CSCE*), Zbigniew Brzezinski urges the U.S. to establish ties with the non-Russian republic governments of the USSR.

July 31, 1991: The U.S. and the USSR sign the Strategic Arms Limitation (hereafter *START-I*) Treaty.

* This chronology was created by Alexander Dillon, Harvard University, with help from Robert De Lossa and supplement by the official chronology of Ukrainian-United States Relations of the Ministry of Foreign Affairs of Ukraine.

August 1, 1991: President Bush in Kyiv warns against "suicidal nationalism" and stresses that the U.S. will support "freedom" in Ukraine but not its independence from the USSR.

August 24, 1991: Following the August *coup d'état* in the USSR, Ukraine declares independence. (Ratified by Parliament on August 28.)

September 25, 1991: During Leonid Kravchuk's visit to Washington, President Bush offers Ukraine such "concessions" as a separate U.S. Peace Corps program for Ukraine in lieu of support for Ukrainian independence.

October 24, 1991: Ukrainian Parliament declares the desire of the Ukrainian nation for eventual non-nuclear status.

October–November 1991: Bills are passed in the House and Senate urging President Bush to extend diplomatic recognition to independent Ukraine.

November 27, 1991: President Bush meets with fifteen Ukrainian-American leaders in the White House and informs them that the Bush administration considers Ukraine "entitled" to independence.

December 1, 1991: The nationwide referendum in Ukraine on Ukrainian independence and the election of Leonid Kuchma as President.

December 8, 1991: The Russian, Belarusian and Ukrainian leaders form the Commonwealth of Independent States (CIS). The U.S. does not extend diplomatic recognition to the new Commonwealth, but does announce that it will continue to work with it on questions of nuclear stability in the lands of the former USSR.

December 18, 1991: U.S. Secretary of State James Baker and Leonid Kravchuk meet. Baker announces that the U.S. considers Ukraine "in the forefront of former Soviet republics seeking U.S. diplomatic recognition," dependent on U.S. concerns about nuclear weapons on Ukrainian soil.

December 25, 1991: President Bush announces formal U.S. diplomatic recognition of independent Ukraine.

1992

January 1992: Ukraine is admitted to the CSCE (later OSCE).

January 23, 1992: Official diplomatic relations between the U.S. and Ukraine are established at a ceremony in the Ministry of Foreign Affairs in Kyiv. (John Gunderson is head of the U.S. consulate general.)

February, 1992: President Kravchuk signs the Helsinki Accords.

February, 1992: Secretary General Manfred Werner invites Ukraine to join NATO's Cooperation Council.

April 11, 1992: Ukrainian Minister of Defense Kostiantyn Morozov visits

Washington at the invitation of Defense Secretary Dick Cheney. Morozov visits military installations.

April 28, 1992: The arrival in Washington of the Ukrainian Ambassador to the U.S., Dr. Oleh Bilorus. (Presents his credentials to President Bush, May 5.)

May 5–11, 1992: President Leonid Kravchuk visits the U.S. for the first time as the President of independent Ukraine. Kravchuk attends the opening ceremony for the Ukrainian Embassy in Washington DC, and meets with President Bush and Secretary of State James Baker. In the course of the talks, Ukraine is given "most favored nation" status by the U.S., eligibility for Oversees Private Development programs, and a separate Peace Corps program for Ukraine. Dr. Yuri Shcherbak, minister for environmental protection, signs first U.S.-Ukraine agreement on environmental collaboration.

May 23, 1992: Ukraine signs the Lisbon Protocol to the START-I Treaty, along with Russia, Belarus and Kazakhstan, and enters the Nuclear Non-proliferation Treaty (NPT). Ukraine does not sign onto the START-I Treaty as a whole, however.

May 25, 1992: U.S. Senate confirmation of Roman Popadiuk (nominated by President Bush, February 6) as the first U.S. ambassador to independent Ukraine.

July 8, 1992: President Kravchuk becomes the first post-Soviet leader to visit NATO headquarters in Brussels.

July 9, 1992: Roman Popadiuk presents his credentials to President Kravchuk.

September 1992: The speaker of the Ukrainian Parliament, Ivan Pliushch visits the U.S. and begins formal relations between the Ukrainian Parliament and the U.S. Congress.

September 1992: The office of the military attaché is opened at the Ukrainian Embassy in Washington.

October 2, 1992: Ukrainian consulate established in Chicago.

October 20, 1992: U.S. Senator Alfonse M. D'Amato (R-NY) calls upon President Bush to issue a proclamation in commemoration of the sixtieth anniversary of the 1932–33 famine in Ukraine.

October 24, 1992: After obtaining congressional approval, President Bush signs into law his bill on "Freedom for Russia and the Emerging Democracies and Open Markets Support Act" (FRIENDSHIP).

1993

January–March 1993: Bilateral talks begin between the Ukrainian Ministry of

Foreign Affairs and the U.S. Department of State to define parameters for mutual cooperation.

February 1993: Ukraine calls for drawing up an amendment to START-I to include a definition of the issue of ownership.

March 23–24, 1993: Ukrainian Minister of Foreign Affairs Anatoliy Zlenko visits U.S. with Ukrainian formulation for the liquidation of nuclear weapons on Ukrainian soil.

April 7, 1993: Working visit of Prime Minister Leonid Kuchma to the U.S. American side expresses displeasure over Ukrainian position on the liquidation of nuclear weapons from Ukrainian territory and refuses high-level talks.

April 1993: U.S. State Department issues declaration of the urgent need for jointly overcoming the "crisis of faith."

May 1993: U.S. Ambassador-at-Large Strobe Talbott meets with President Kravchuk in Ukraine. To help move the START-I ratification process along, he affirms U.S. commitment to Ukraine's international security, but also stresses that the nuclear issue should not dominate U.S.-Ukrainian relations.

June 6–7, 1993: Secretary of Defense Les Aspen visits Ukraine to discuss security matters. Makes proposals concerning dismantling Ukrainian nuclear weapons to be followed closely by dismantling Russian ones, reimbursing Ukraine for the uranium, and the possibility of sealing U.S. commitment to Ukraine's security by means of a charter of U.S.-Ukrainian relations.

June 12, 1993: President Clinton telephones President Kravchuk. Again reaffirms U.S. commitment to Ukrainian security concerns.

July 7–9, 1993: Senator Mitch McConnell (R-KY) visits Kyiv. Announcement concerning the need for the U.S. Congress to give separate aid to Ukraine.

July 10, 1993: U.S. Ambassador to Ukraine Roman Popadiuk condemns the Russian Duma's statements regarding the status of Sevastopol.

July 25–30, 1993: Defense Minister Morozov visits the U.S. and signs a memorandum of understanding on cooperation and communications between the Ukrainian Ministry of Defense and the U.S. Department of Defense.

September 1993: A U.S. foreign aid bill is signed into law for $2.3 billion in assistance to newly independent states (NIS). Due to pressure from the U.S. Congress throughout the preceding summer, the portion earmarked by the bill specifically for Ukraine is raised to 330 million dollars.

October 1993: Visit to the U.S. of the president of the Ukrainian Academy of Agricultural Sciences, O. O. Sozinov. Cooperative agreements signed between Beltsville Agricultural Research Center (U.S. Department of Agriculture, Maryland) and the Ukrainian National Library of Agriculture.

October 4–6, 1993: Official visit of Foreign Minister Anatoliy Zlenko to the U.S. for talks on industrial-economic and scientific-technical cooperation.

October 13, 1993: William Miller takes oath as new U.S. Ambassador to Ukraine, replacing Roman Popadiuk. (Presents his credentials on October 20.)

October 24–25, 1993: Secretary of State Warren Christopher visits Ukraine and tries to persuade Ukraine to unilaterally disarm and commit to the START-I Treaty. He also offers assistance money for the dismantling.

November 18, 1993: The Ukrainian parliament ratifies the START-I Treaty and Lisbon Protocols, but with 13 conditions attached, including firmer U.S. commitments to Ukrainian security and assistance in dismantling the warheads. President Clinton expresses disappointment in a telephone call to President Kravchuk.

December 1993: "Nationalist-communist" victory in Russian parliamentary elections, which contributes to a gradual "pro-Ukrainian" shift in U.S. diplomacy.

1994

January 4–7, 1994: Working visit of Vice-Prime Minister Valeriy Shmarov to the U.S., with preliminary agreement on the most important aspects on Ukrainian nuclear disarmament.

January 12, 1994: President Clinton, on his way to Moscow, stops in Kyiv for three hours as a gesture of goodwill towards Ukraine and incentive for Ukraine to maintain its commitment to the disarmament process.

January 14, 1994: In Moscow, Presidents Clinton, Kravchuk, and Yeltsin sign the "Trilateral Agreement" on denuclearization. In return for destruction of missiles and warheads, Ukraine gets monetary and technical assistance and Russia forgives Ukrainian debt.

January 24–28, 1994: Minister of the Economy Roman Shpek visits the U.S. to discuss concrete proposals for bilateral and multilateral economic cooperation.

February 3, 1994: Ukrainian parliament drops its earlier reservations and ratifies the START-I Treaty and the Lisbon Protocol.

February 8, 1994: Ukraine joins NATO's Partnership for Peace (PfP), becoming the first post-Soviet country to do so.

March 3–7, 1994: President Kravchuk visits the U.S. The U.S. government aid to Ukraine is doubled to $700 million, U.S. extends its Generalized System of Preference (GSP) status to Ukraine, and Kravchuk and Clinton sign a joint statement on U.S.-Ukrainian Friendship and Cooperation. Clinton assures Ukraine that the U.S. will offer security assurances once the START-I Treaty comes into effect and Ukraine joins the NPT.

March 21–23, 1994: During a visit to Ukraine, U.S. Defense Secretary William Perry promises $100 million in aid for the denuclearization and military conversion process.

May 1994: The CSCE holds hearings on the issue of the U.S.' relations with Russia and the post-Soviet states. There is some criticism of the U.S.' apparent preferences for Russia over Ukraine and other post-Soviet states.

May 2–5, 1994: Visit to Kyiv of U.S. economic delegation to Ukraine headed by Nicholas Burns, during which U.S. assistance for economic reform in Ukraine is discussed.

June 13–19, 1994: Visit of Defense Minister Vitaliy Radetskyi to the U.S., with agreements reached on broadening military cooperation.

July 8–10. 1994: The Group of Seven industrialized nations (G-7) promise $4.2 billion in aid to help Ukraine qualify for future IMF and World-Bank loans and to facilitate the shutdown of Chornobyl.

August 2, 1994: U.S. Vice-President Al Gore visits Kyiv to affirm continued U.S. support for Ukraine and for the new president Leonid Kuchma, elected on July 10.

August 10–11, 1994: Assistant Secretary of State James Collins heads a high-level U.S. delegation to Kyiv to work on plans for future economic cooperation and security programs.

September 4–14, 1994: Deputy Chairman of the Ukrainian Parliament, Oleksandr Dyomin visits U.S. to discuss privatization, ownership of land, housing, and defense industry conversion.

September 29–October 5, 1994: Oleksandr Moroz, Chairman of the Parliament, visits the U.S. to broaden and deepen ties between the Ukrainian Parliament and the U.S. Congress.

October 21, 1994: Yuri Shcherbak, formerly Ukrainian ambassador to Israel, is appointed ambassador to the U.S., replacing Oleh Bilorus. (Shcherbak presents his credentials to President Clinton on November 21.)

October 1994: The G-7 nations pledge a $1.2 billion aid package to Ukraine at a conference in Winnipeg, Canada.

November 13–16, 1994: Vice-Prime Minister and Minister of Defense Valeriy Shmarov visits U.S. to formalize the mechanism and aims of aid to Ukraine through the Nunn-Lugar Act.

November 18, 1994: Ukrainian Parliament accedes to the NPT, though expresses desire for greater security assurances from the West.

November 19–23, 1994: President Leonid Kuchma visits the U.S. On November 22 he and Clinton sign "Charter for Ukrainian-American Partnership, Friendship and Cooperation." The U.S. announces aid to Ukraine of $350 million. In all 14 bilateral agreements signed.

December 5, 1994: Kuchma signs Ukraine onto the NPT at a CSCE summit in Budapest. The U.S., Great Britain, and Russia offer Ukraine security assurances.

1995

January 9, 1995: Minister of Communications O. Prozhyval'skyi visits U.S. and signs memorandum of mutual understanding in the area of telecommunications.

March 31–April 1, 1995: Defense Secretary William Perry goes to Ukraine and moves past issues of nuclear disarmament to questions of social protection, security and military and economic cooperation. Secretary Perry watches destruction of an SS-19 missile in Pervomaiske.

April 10, 1995: Visit of Deputy Secretary of State Strobe Talbott to Kyiv, with discussions of further bilateral relations.

April 30–May 2, 1995: Secretary of the Ukrainian National Security Council Volodymyr Horbulin visits U.S. to discuss broad range of bilateral issues.

May 1995: Ukrainian Minister of Environmental Protection Iu. Kostenko visits U.S. and signs a joint memorandum with the NRC in the area of nuclear safety.

May 1995: Defense Secretary William Perry goes to Yavoriv to review "Peace Shield '95," the first U.S.-Ukraine joint peacekeeping exercise under the PfP program. 2-week training exercise.

May 11–12, 1995: State visit of President Bill Clinton and Hillary Rodham Clinton.

July 1995: Ukrainian head of the State Nuclear Committee M. Umanets visits U.S. to explore possibility of manufacturing nuclear fuel in Ukraine.

August 1995: Ukrainian Marine brigade visits U.S. Marine training installations.

September 1995: Ukraine signs agreement with NATO on possible "participation in some of its structures" (as expressed by Hennadiy Udovenko), in accordance with the 16+1 formula.

September 1995: Senate's version of Foreign Assistance Appropriations Act for Fiscal Year 1996 includes $225 million earmark for Ukraine, championed by Sen. Mitch McConnell (chairman of Senate Appropriations Committee Subcommittee on Foreign Operations). (Adopted October 24.)

September 25–29, 1995: Official visit of Prime Minister Yevhen Marchuk to the U.S.

October 21–24, 1995: Ukrainian President Kuchma visits New York to take part in 50th anniversary celebrations of the founding of the UN. Meets with President Clinton.

December 20, 1995: Ukraine and G-7 members signs Memorandum of Understanding in Ottawa. Ukraine agrees to decommission Chernobyl Atomic Energy Station by 2000. In return, the G-7 nations pledge $2.3 billion to Ukraine in assistance.

1996

January 4–5, 1996: Defense Secretary William Perry visits Ukraine. Signs agreement with Ukrainian Defense Minister Valeriy Shmarov on closer military cooperation between U.S. and Ukraine. Discuss NATO expansion and possibility of trilateral military training exercises during meeting with Shmarov and Grachev. Also meets with President Kuchma.

January 5, 1996: Secretary Perry, Minister Shmarov, and Russian Defense Minister Pavel Grachev go to Pervomaiske, Mikolaïv Oblast, Ukraine to watch destruction of an ICBM missile silo. (The third of 130 to be dismantled by November 1998, according to START-I treaty.)

January 26, 1996: President Clinton signs Foreign Assistance Appropriations Act for Fiscal Year 1996 in law. Makes Ukraine third largest recipient of foreign aid after Israel and Egypt. $12.1 billion legislation mandated at least $225 million for Ukraine and at most $195 million for Russia. Congress earmarks $75 million over the 1995 levels for Ukraine in 1996 on condition of continued economic reforms, despite the trend of overall cuts in foreign aid.

February 20–22, 1996: President Kuchma visits Washington (for 2nd time since taking office in July 1994). President Clinton assures continued U.S. support for Ukraine's economic reforms. Meets also Secretary of State Warren Christopher, Secretary of Defense William Perry, and Treasury Secretary Robert Rubin.

February 21, 1996: Kuchma presented with 1996 Freedom award for "contribution to world peace, regional security and inter-ethnic cooperation" by Freedom House, the human rights watchdog organization.

March 1996: Ukrainian state delegations for energy conservation, coal industry, and airspace visit Washington for talks with U.S. counterparts.

March 19–20, 1996: U.S. Secretary of State Warren Christopher visits Kyiv. Christopher condemns the decision of the Russian Duma to declare the dissolution of the USSR illegal.

April 15, 1996: First ever visit by a NATO chief to Ukraine. NATO Secretary General Javier Solana visits Kyiv, during which Foreign Minister Hennadiy Udovenko emphasizes that relations between Ukraine and NATO include Ukraine's participation in PfP program, its involvement in NATO's Cooperation Council, commitment to peacekeeping with IFOR troops in Bosnia.

April 21, 1996: During G-7 summit on Nuclear Safety and Security in Moscow, President Kuchma formally agrees to close Chernobyl by 2000 in exchange for $3.1 billion in assistance from G-7.

May 2, 1996: U.S.-Ukraine trade ties expanded with opening of West Coast Regional Office of Ukrainian Embassy's Trade and Economic Mission in Los Angeles by Ambassador Shcherbak. (The other three are in Washington, DC, New York, and Chicago.)

June 1–10: U.S. troops from 1st Infantry Division and Ukraine's 24th Mechanized Rifle Division hold joint peacekeeping exercises in Lviv at a training area. Called "Peace shield '96." (Peace Shield 95 took place in Yavoriv, and Peace Shield II was in Kansas.)

July 8–14, 1996: Roman Shpek, chairman of the State Commission for Reconstruction and Development, visits the U.S. to engage in bilateral talks on development, the IMF, and the World Bank.

July 17–18, 1996: Deputy Secretary of State Talbott in Kyiv meets with President Kuchma, Prime Minister Pavlo Lazarenko, Chairman of Parliament Oleksandr Moroz, Foreign Affairs Minister Hennadiy Udovenko, and National Security and Defense Council Secretary Volodymyr Horbulin. They discuss ways of strengthening bilateral relationships.

July 25, 1996: Prime Minister Pavlo Lazarenko's first working visit to Washington. Meets with U.S. Congressional and governmental leaders, IMF and World Bank. Assures them that Ukraine will continue economic reforms.

July 26, 1996: Minister Udovenko (a member of the PM's delegation) meets separately with Deputy Secretary of State Talbott. Discusses creation of a Kuchma-Gore commission (analogous to the Gore-Chernomyrdin Commission). Passes letter to Secretary of State Christopher outlining Ukraine's proposal for creation of a nuclear-free zone in Central and Eastern Europe.

July 16, 1996: Senate approves Foreign Assistance Appropriations Act for FY 1997 with $225 million earmark for Ukraine. Bill then moves to House-

Senate conference committee to iron out differences between House and Senate versions. (House version has no earmark for Ukraine.)

August 1, 1996: Rep Benjamin Gilman (R-NY), chairman of House International Relations Committee, reintroduces Concurrent Resolution 120 "supporting the Independence and Sovereignty of Ukraine and its Political and Economic Reforms"—first time ever such a resolution entered in Congress. (Initially proposed December 1995.) Urges Ukrainian government to continue democratic and economic reforms and calls on president of U.S. to support U.S. security assistance for Ukraine and to insist that government of Russian Federation recognize Ukraine sovereignty. (Passed by House, September 4; passed by Senate September 18.)

August 27–29, 1996: Senator Richard Lugar (R-IN) visits Kyiv.

September 16–19, 1996: Secretary of National Security and Defense Council of Ukraine Horbulin meets with Deputy Secretary of State Talbott, Defense Secretary Perry, National Security Advisor Anthony Lake, CIA Director John Deutsch and FBI Assistant Director William Esposito in Washington on a four-day visit. Finalize details of Kuchma-Gore commission, discuss creation of collective security system in Europe, Ukraine's relationship with NATO, and possibility of Ukraine joining Missile Technology Control Regime.

September 17, 1996: House-Senate Conference Committee on the Foreign Assistance Appropriations Act resolves all but one difference between House and Senate versions of the bill. $625 million is appropriated for NIS, with $225 million earmarked for Ukraine. (Signed into law by Clinton, September 30.)

September 19, 1996: White House officially announces creation of the Kuchma-Gore Commission, named the U.S.-Ukraine Binational Commission. President Kuchma and Vice-President Gore to chair the commission and will meet annually to discuss its work. It will have four committees: Foreign Policy, Security, Trade and Investment, and Sustainable Economic Cooperation.

September 27–October 4, 1996: Vice-Prime Minister Volodymyr Pynzenyk arrives in Washington at the head of a delegation to take part in the annual meetings of the IMF and World Bank.

October 10–11, 1996: Meeting of U.S.-Ukraine Coordinating Committee in Kyiv. Resolutions adopted concerning the development of Ukrainian-American relations in the areas of security, economy (especially in energy), and informational and cultural ties. A recommendation is made that Ukraine have the closest possible ties with NATO structures.

October 14–16, 1996: First meeting of the Kuchma-Gore Commission Committee on Sustainable Economic Cooperation.

October 21–22, 1996: Foreign Affairs Minister Hennadiy Udovenko meets Secretary of State Christopher, Deputy Secretary of State Talbott, Defense Secretary Perry, and Deputy National Security Advisor Sandy Berger during visit to Washington. Discusses expansion of NATO. Udovenko reiterates Ukraine's position that NATO expansion be evolutionary, that NATO strengthen relations with Ukraine as it expands, and that NATO not introduce nuclear weapons onto the territory of new members.

October 22, 1996: President Clinton formally announces that NATO will expand to include the first group of East European countries in 1999.

November 4, 1996: First meeting of the Kuchma-Gore Commission Committee on Security, in Washington.

November 5–6, 1996: First meeting of the Kuchma-Gore Commission Committee on Foreign Policy, in Washington.

December 10, 1996: NATO member states meeting in Brussels declare that NATO has no plans to deploy nuclear weapons on territories of its new member states (which states will be announced next summer).

December 17–19, 1996: Vice-Prime Minister Volodymyr Pynzenyk leads working mission to a meeting of the Consultative Group of Donor Nations to Ukraine, at which time he affirms Ukraine's commitment to the reform process within the parameters of a three-year IMF (EFF) program.

1997

February 10–14, 1997: Ukrainian Minister of Environmental Protection Yu. Kostenko leads a governmental delegation to the "G-7" countries, to discuss the closure of the Chornobyl Nuclear Power Plant.

March 1997: Secretary of the National Security and Defense Council Volodymyr Horbulin and Ukrainian Foreign Minister Hennadiy Udovenko negotiate with leaders of NATO in Brussels concerning the Ukrainian-NATO relationship. This is in preparation for the July 1997 NATO summit in Madrid. Udovenko goes on to Washington to meet with Secretary of State Madeleine Albright to prepare for the upcoming visit of President Leonid Kuchma to the U.S. and to prepare for the first plenary session of the Kuchma-Gore Commission.

April 1997: Visit to Ukraine of Ambassador Richard Morningstar, Clinton's special advisor and Deputy Secretary of State on assistance to the NIS countries, in preparation for President Kuchma's visit to Washington in May.

April 28–May 2, 1997: First visit of Ukrainian Minister of Defense Col.-Gen. Oleksandr Kuzmuk to the U.S. Meets with Secretary of Defense William Cohen. Ukraine receives $47 million of assistance to dismantle nuclear missile silos and transportation facilities/devices.

May 7, 1997: A one-day visit of NATO Secretary General Javier Solana to Kyiv. He presides over the opening of a NATO Information Center in Kyiv. He also presents President Kuchma with a draft agreement on NATO-Ukrainian relations to be signed at the July NATO summit in Madrid.

May 14–16, 1997: Working visit of President Kuchma and major government ministers to the U.S. Meets with Al Gore to discuss the work of the Kuchma-Gore commission. First plenary session of the Kuchma-Gore Commission.

June 6, 1997: First Vice-Prime Minister Vasyl Durdinets and Minister of Internal Affairs Yuriy Kravchenko hold formal talks with FBI Director Louis J. Freeh, Assistant to the Vice-President for National Security Leon Fuerth, National Security Council Director Carlos Pascual, and Assistant Secretary of State Stuart E. Eizenstat in Washington.

June 22–23, 1997: President Kuchma participates in special sessions of the UN on the environment. Conducts working visit with Vice-President Gore during the visit.

July 9, 1997: Presidents Kuchma and Clinton are among the signatories of a special charter defining the relationship between NATO and Ukraine. (See appendix 2.)

July 11–12, 1997: Official visit of Secretary of Defense Cohen to Ukraine to discuss prospects for military cooperation. Secretary Cohen visits the joint military exercises "Cooperative Neighbor–97," and meets with Secretary Horbulin and heads of the Ukrainian defense ministry.

September 21–23, 1997: President Kuchma addresses the fifty-second session of the UN General Assembly and privately meets with President Clinton and Secretary of State Albright.

October 20–21, 1997: Third meeting of the Kuchma-Gore Commission's Committee on Sustainable Economic Cooperation, in Kyiv.

October 23, 1997: Third meeting of the Kuchma-Gore Commission's Committee on Security, in Washington.

November 16, 1997: Goodwill visit by First Lady Hillary Clinton to Lviv.

November 19, 1997: President Kuchma attends the launch of the space-shuttle "Columbia" with a Ukrainian astronaut, Leonid Kadenyuk, on board. President Kuchma and NASA Administrator Daniel Goldin discussed the possibilities for further development of Ukrainian-U.S. cooperation in space research.

November 20, 1997: President Kuchma and Vice-President Gore co-chair the Conference of Donors on the Shelter Implementation Plan. The international community assures Ukraine of its assistance for the transformation of the shelter (the Chornobyl "Sarcophogus") into an environmentally safe structure.

November 20, 1997: President Kuchma and Vice-President Gore hold informal talks on a wide range of issues of bilateral cooperation.

November 21, 1997: Secretary Horbulin visits Washington to discuss further bilateral and multilateral cooperation under the NATO-Ukraine Charter as well as non-proliferation issues and Ukraine-U.S. military cooperation in both political and technical issues.

Charter on a Distinctive Partnership Between the North Atlantic Treaty Organization and Ukraine

Madrid, 9 July 1997

I. Building an Enhanced NATO-Ukraine Relationship

The North Atlantic Treaty Organization (NATO) and its member States and Ukraine, hereinafter referred to as NATO and Ukraine,

— building on a political commitment at the highest level;

— recognizing the fundamental changes in the security environment in Europe which have inseparably linked the security of every state to that of all the others;

— determined to strengthen mutual trust and cooperation in order to enhance security and stability, and to cooperate in building a stable, peaceful and undivided Europe;

— stressing the profound transformation undertaken by NATO since the end of the Cold War and its continued adaptation to meet the changing circumstances of Euro-Atlantic security, including its support, on a case-by-case basis, of new missions of peacekeeping operations carried out under the authority of the United Nations Security Council or the responsibility of the OSCE;

— welcoming the progress achieved by Ukraine and looking forward to further steps to develop its democratic institutions, to implement radical economic reforms, and to deepen the process of integration with the full range of European and Euro-Atlantic structures;

— noting NATO's positive role in maintaining peace and stability in Europe and in promoting greater confidence and transparency in the

Euro-Atlantic area, and its openness for cooperation with the new democracies of Central and Eastern Europe, an inseparable part of which is Ukraine;

— convinced that an independent, democratic and stable Ukraine is one of the key factors for ensuring stability in Central and Eastern Europe, and the continent as a whole;

— mindful of the importance of a strong and enduring relationship between NATO and Ukraine and recognizing the solid progress made, across a broad range of activities, to develop an enhanced and strengthened relationship between NATO and Ukraine on the foundations created by the Joint Press Statement of 14 September 1995;

— determined to further expand and intensify their cooperation in the framework of the Euro-Atlantic Partnership Council, including the enhanced Partnership for Peace program;

— welcoming their practical cooperation within IFOR/SFOR and other peacekeeping operations on the territory of the former Yugoslavia;

— sharing the view that the opening of the Alliance to new members, in accordance with Article 10 of the Washington Treaty, is directed at enhancing the stability of Europe, and the security of all countries in Europe without recreating dividing lines;

are committed, on the basis of this Charter, to further broaden and strengthen their cooperation and to develop a distinctive and effective partnership, which will promote further stability and common democratic values in Central and Eastern Europe.

II. Principles for the Development of NATO-Ukraine Relations

NATO and Ukraine will base their relationship on the principles, obligations and commitments under international law and international instruments, including the United Nations Charter, the Helsinki Final Act and subsequent OSCE documents. Accordingly, NATO and Ukraine reaffirm their commitment to:

— the recognition that security of all states in the OSCE area is indivisible, that no state should pursue its security at the expense of that of another state, and that no state can regard any part of the OSCE region as its sphere of influence;

— refrain from the threat or use of force against any state in any manner inconsistent with the United Nations Charter or Helsinki Final Act principles guiding participating States;

— the inherent right of all states to choose and to implement freely their own security arrangements, and to be free to choose or change their security arrangements, including treaties of alliance, as they evolve;

— respect for the sovereignty, territorial integrity and political independence of all other states, for the inviolability of frontiers, and the development of good-neighborly relations;

— the rule of law, the fostering of democracy, political pluralism and a market economy;

— human rights and the rights of persons belonging to national minorities;

— the prevention of conflicts and settlement of disputes by peaceful means in accordance with UN and OSCE principles.

Ukraine reaffirms its determination to carry forward its defense reforms, to strengthen democratic and civilian control of the armed forces, and to increase their interoperability with the forces of NATO and Partner countries. NATO reaffirms its support for Ukraine's efforts in these areas. Ukraine welcomes NATO's continuing and active adaptation to meet the changing circumstances of Euro-Atlantic security, and its role, in cooperation with other international organizations such as the OSCE, the European Union, the Council of Europe and the Western European Union in promoting Euro-Atlantic security and fostering a general climate of trust and confidence in Europe.

III. Areas for Consultation and/or Cooperation between NATO and Ukraine

Reaffirming the common goal of implementation of a broad range of issues for consultation and cooperation, NATO and Ukraine commit themselves to develop and strengthen their consultation and/or cooperation in the areas described below. In this regard, NATO and Ukraine reaffirm their commitment to the full development of the EAPC and the enhanced PFP. This includes Ukrainian participation in operations, including peacekeeping operations, on a case-by-case basis, under the authority of the UN Security Council, or the responsibility of the OSCE, and, if CJTF are used in such cases, Ukrainian participation in them at an early stage on a case-by-case basis, subject to decisions by the North Atlantic Council on specific operations.

Consultations between NATO and Ukraine will cover issues of common concern, such as:

— political and security related subjects, in particular the development of Euro-Atlantic security and stability, including the security of Ukraine;

— conflict prevention, crisis management, peace support, conflict resolution and humanitarian operations, taking into account the roles of the United Nations and the OSCE in this field;

— the political and defense aspects of nuclear, biological and chemical non-proliferation;

— disarmament and arms control issues, including those related to the Treaty on Conventional Armed Forces in Europe (CFE Treaty), the Open Skies Treaty and confidence and security building measures in the 1994 Vienna Document;

— arms exports and related technology transfers;

— combating drug-trafficking and terrorism.

Areas for consultation and cooperation, in particular through joint seminars, joint working groups, and other cooperative programs, will cover a broad range of topics, such as:

— civil emergency planning, and disaster preparedness;

— civil-military relations, democratic control of the armed forces, and Ukrainian defense reform;

— defense planning, budgeting, policy, strategy and national security concepts;

— defense conversion;

— NATO-Ukraine military cooperation and interoperability;

— economic aspects of security;

— science and technology issues;

— environmental security issues, including nuclear safety;

— aerospace research and development, through AGARD;

— civil-military coordination of air traffic management and control.

In addition, NATO and Ukraine will explore to the broadest possible degree the following areas for cooperation:

— armaments cooperation (beyond the existing CNAD dialogue);

— military training, including PFP exercises on Ukrainian territory and NATO support for the Polish-Ukrainian peacekeeping battalion;

— promotion of defense cooperation between Ukraine and its neighbors.

Other areas for consultation and cooperation may be added, by mutual agreement, on the basis of experience gained.

Given the importance of information activities to improve reciprocal knowledge and understanding, NATO has established an Information and Documentation Centre in Kyiv. The Ukrainian side will provide its full support to the operation of the Centre in accordance with the Memorandum of Understanding between NATO and the Government of Ukraine signed at Kyiv on 7 May 1997.

IV. Practical Arrangements for Consultation and Cooperation
between NATO and Ukraine

Consultation and cooperation as set out in this Charter will be implemented through:

— NATO-Ukraine meetings at the level of the North Atlantic Council at intervals to be mutually agreed;

— NATO-Ukraine meetings with appropriate NATO Committees as mutually agreed;

— reciprocal high-level visits;

— mechanisms for military cooperation, including periodic meetings with NATO Chiefs of Defense and activities within the framework of the enhanced Partnership for Peace programme;

— a military liaison mission of Ukraine will be established as part of a Ukrainian mission to NATO in Brussels. NATO retains the right reciprocally to establish a NATO military liaison mission in Kyiv.

Meetings will normally take place at NATO Headquarters in Brussels. Under exceptional circumstances, they may be convened elsewhere, including in Ukraine, as mutually agreed. Meetings, as a rule, will take place on the basis of an agreed calendar.

NATO and Ukraine consider their relationship as an evolving, dynamic process. To ensure that they are developing their relationship and implementing the provisions of this Charter to the fullest extent possible, the North Atlantic Council will periodically meet with Ukraine as the NATO-Ukraine Commission, as a rule not less than twice a year. The NATO-Ukraine Commission will not duplicate the functions of other mechanisms described in this Charter, but instead would meet to assess broadly the implementation of the relationship, survey planning for the future, and suggest ways to improve or further develop cooperation between NATO and Ukraine.

NATO and Ukraine will encourage expanded dialogue and cooperation between the North Atlantic Assembly and the Verkhovna Rada.

V. Cooperation for a More Secure Europe

NATO Allies will continue to support Ukrainian sovereignty and independence, territorial integrity, democratic development, economic prosperity and its status as a non-nuclear weapon state, and the principle of inviolability of frontiers, as key factors of stability and security in Central and Eastern Europe and in the continent as a whole. NATO and Ukraine will develop a crisis consultative mechanism to consult together whenever Ukraine perceives a direct threat to its territorial integrity, political independence, or security.

NATO welcomes and supports the fact that Ukraine received security assurances from all five nuclear-weapon states parties to the Treaty on the Non-Proliferation of Nuclear Weapons (NPT) as a non-nuclear weapon state party to the NPT, and recalls the commitments undertaken by the United States and the United Kingdom, together with Russia, and by France unilaterally, which took the historic decision in Budapest in 1994 to provide Ukraine with security assurances as a non-nuclear weapon state party to the NPT. Ukraine's landmark decision to renounce nuclear weapons and to accede to the NPT as a non-nuclear weapon state greatly contributed to the strengthening of security and stability in Europe and has earned Ukraine special stature in the world community. NATO welcomes Ukraine's decision to support the indefinite extension of the NPT and its contribution to the withdrawal and dismantlement of nuclear weapons which were based on its territory. Ukraine's strengthened cooperation with NATO will enhance and deepen the political dialogue between Ukraine and the members of the Alliance on a broad range of security matters, including on nuclear issues. This will contribute to the improvement of the overall security environment in Europe. NATO and Ukraine note the entry into force of the CFE Flank Document on 15 May 1997. NATO and Ukraine will continue to cooperate on issues of mutual interest such as CFE adaptation. NATO and Ukraine intend to improve the operation of the CFE treaty in a changing environment and, through that, the security of each state party, irrespective of whether it belongs to a political-military alliance. They share the view that the presence of foreign troops on the territory of a participating state must be in conformity with international law, the freely expressed consent of the host state or a relevant decision of the United Nations Security Council. Ukraine welcomes the statement by NATO members that "enlarging the Alliance will not require a change in NATO's current nuclear posture and, therefore, NATO countries have no intention, no plan and no reason to deploy nuclear weapons on the territory of new members nor any need to change any aspect of NATO's nuclear posture or nuclear policy — and do not foresee any future need to do so."

NATO member States and Ukraine will continue fully to implement all agreements on disarmament, non-proliferation and arms control and confidence-building measures they are part of.

The present Charter takes effect upon its signature.

The present Charter is established in two originals in the English, French, and Ukrainian languages, all three texts having equal validity.

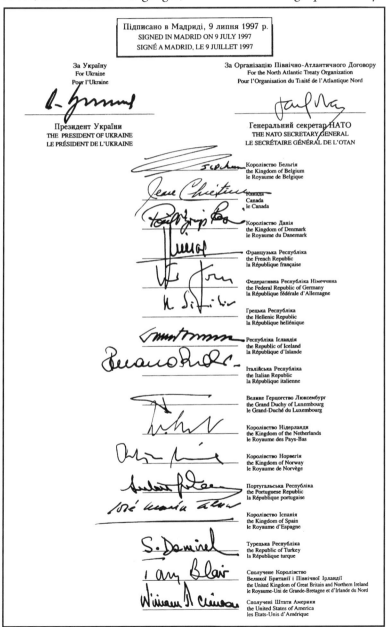

Підписано в Мадриді, 9 липня 1997 р.
SIGNED IN MADRID ON 9 JULY 1997
SIGNÉ A MADRID, LE 9 JUILLET 1997

За Україну
For Ukraine
Pour l'Ukraine

За Організацію Північно-Атлантичного Договору
For the North Atlantic Treaty Organization
Pour l'Organisation du Traité de l'Atlantique Nord

Президент України
THE PRESIDENT OF UKRAINE
LE PRÉSIDENT DE L'UKRAINE

Генеральний секретар НАТО
THE NATO SECRETARY GENERAL
LE SECRÉTAIRE GÉNÉRAL DE L'OTAN

Королівство Бельгія
the Kingdom of Belgium
le Royaume de Belgique

Канада
Canada
le Canada

Королівство Данія
the Kingdom of Denmark
le Royaume du Danemark

Французька Республіка
the French Republic
la République française

Федеративна Республіка Німеччина
the Federal Republic of Germany
la République fédérale d'Allemagne

Грецька Республіка
the Hellenic Republic
la République hellénique

Республіка Ісландія
the Republic of Iceland
la République d'Islande

Італійська Республіка
the Italian Republic
la République italienne

Велике Герцогство Люксембург
the Grand Duchy of Luxembourg
le Grand-Duché du Luxembourg

Королівство Нідерланди
the Kingdom of the Netherlands
le Royaume des Pays-Bas

Королівство Норвегія
the Kingdom of Norway
le Royaume de Norvège

Португальська Республіка
the Portuguese Republic
la République portugaise

Королівство Іспанія
the Kingdom of Spain
le Royaume d'Espagne

Турецька Республіка
the Republic of Turkey
la République turque

Сполучене Королівство
Великої Британії і Північної Ірландії
the United Kingdom of Great Britain and Northern Ireland
le Royaume-Uni de Grande-Bretagne et d'Irlande du Nord

Сполучені Штати Америки
the United States of America
les Etats-Unis d'Amérique

About the Author

Dr. Yuri Shcherbak was born in Kyiv on October 12, 1934. He graduated from Kyiv Medical College in 1958, and has both Ph.D. and D.Sc. degrees in epidemiology. He is a member of the National Academy of Environmental Sciences of Ukraine.

Dr. Shcherbak began his active political career in 1989 when he won a seat in the USSR Supreme Soviet, where he was a close associate of Dr. Andrei Sakharov. As an opposition leader and chairman of the subcommittee on energy and nuclear safety, Dr. Shcherbak initiated and led the first parliamentary investigation of the Chornobyl accident and the nuclear catastrophes in Semipalatinsk and in the Urals. Never having been affiliated with the Soviet Communist Party, he founded and became the leader of the Ukrainian Green Movement in 1988 (it became the Green Party in 1990). In 1991, he was appointed minister of environmental protection of Ukraine, and a member of the National Security Council. He was Ukraine's first ambassador to Israel in 1992 and remained in that post until November, 1994, when he was appointed Ukraine's Ambassador to the United States. He presented his credentials to President Bill Clinton on November 21, 1994, during the state visit of President Leonid Kuchma to Washington, D.C. In 1997 he was appointed Ukraine's first ambassador to Mexico (concurrent with his service as ambassador to the United States) and presented his credentials on September 10, 1997 to President Ernesto Zedillo.

An eyewitness to the 1986 Chornobyl nuclear disaster, Dr. Shcherbak wrote the sensational exposé documentary novel *Chornobyl*, which has been printed in most of the former Soviet republics and also in the West. The novel was published in English in 1989. Dr. Shcherbak also wrote extensively on the Stalinist man-made famine in Ukraine in 1932–33. As a writer, Yuri Shcherbak is a well-known novelist who has authored 20 books of prose, plays, poetry, and essays. He is a member of Ukraine's Writers' Union and Cinematographers' Union, and was on the executive board of the Writers' Union from 1987 to 1989. He has been awarded medals and prizes in literature, medicine, and for his work as a Ukrainian statesman.

Ambassador Shcherbak has been married to his wife, Maria, for 38 years and has two children, an older son, Jaroslav, who is a physician with a Ph.D. in cardiology, and a younger daughter, Bohdana, also a physician, who specializes in pediatrics.

Ukrainian Research Institute
Harvard University
Selected Publications

Political Communities and Gendered Ideologies in Contemporary Ukraine (The Petryshyn Memorial Lecture, Harvard University, 26 April 1994). Martha Bohachevsky-Chomiak. Harvard Papers in Ukrainian Studies. Softcover, ISBN 0-916458-72-5.

The Great Soviet Peasant War. Bolsheviks and Peasants, 1917–1933. Andrea Graziosi. Harvard Papers in Ukrainian Studies. Softcover, ISBN 0-916458-83-0.

Carpatho-Ukraine in the Twentieth Century: A Political and Legal History. Vincent Shandor. URI Publications. Clothbound, ISBN 0-916458-86-5.

The Military Tradition in Ukrainian History: Its Role in the Construction of Ukraine's Armed Forces. Kostiantyn P. Morozov, et al. Harvard Papers in Ukrainian Studies. Softcover, ISBN 0-916458-73-3.

Ukrainian Futurism, 1914–1930: A Historical and Critical Study. Oleh S. Ilnytzkyj. Harvard Series in Ukrainian Studies. Clothbound, ISBN 0-916458-56-3. Softcover, ISBN 0-916458-59-8.

Kistiakovsky: The Struggle for National and Constitutional Rights in the Last Years of Tsarism. Susan Heuman. Harvard Series in Ukrainian Studies. Clothbound, ISBN 0-916458-61-X.

To receive a free catalogue of all Ukrainian Research Institute publications (including the journal *Harvard Ukrainian Studies*) please write, fax, or call to:

URI Publications
1583 Massachusetts Avenue
Cambridge, MA 02138
USA
tel. 617-495-3692 *fax.* 617-495-8097

e-mail:
huri@fas.harvard.edu
on-line catalog:
http://www.sabre.org/huri (follow the publications path)